TEN COMMANDMENTS

for Pastors New to a Congregation

TEN COMMANDMENTS

for Pastors New to a Congregation

Lawrence W. Farris

William B. Eerdmans Publishing Company

Grand Rapids, Michigan / Cambridge, U.K.

© 2003 Wm. B. Eerdmans Publishing Co.

Wm. B. Eerdmans Publishing Co.
2140 Oak Industrial Drive N.E., Grand Rapids, Michigan 49505 /
P.O. Box 163, Cambridge CB3 9PU U.K.

Printed in the United States of America

12 11 10 09 08 07   9 8 7 6 5 4 3

Library of Congress Cataloging-in-Publication Data

Farris, Lawrence W.
Ten commandments for pastors new to a congregation /
Lawrence W. Farris.
p.   cm.
Includes index.
ISBN 978-0-8028-2128-7 (pbk.)
1. Pastoral theology.   I. Title.
BV4011.3.F37   2003
253 — dc22

2003059649

www.eerdmans.com

In Gratitude to

The Reverend Garnett E. Foster

Partner in Theological Dialogue
Finder of Extraordinary Restaurants
Witness for Justice and Peace

Contents

• CONTENTS •

Acknowledgments

I am most grateful to the congregations with which I have been a new pastor at various points in my ministry: the First Presbyterian Church of Annapolis, Maryland; the Okemos Presbyterian Church, Okemos, Michigan; and the First Presbyterian Church of Three Rivers-Centreville, Michigan. The good and gracious people of the Annapolis church were particularly skilled and patient as I learned the many lessons my seminary work had not covered. Their shaping of me as well as a number of other right-out-of-seminary associate pastors has served the larger church well. The Reverend Winslow D. Shaw, a longtime pastor of that congregation, really should be the author of this book as his expertise as a mentor to new pastors was unsurpassed.

It has been my privilege, and usually my joy, to mentor, both formally and informally, several pastors new to congregations from a number of faith traditions. While their names have been changed in the pages that follow, and some incidents they related to me conflated, their experiences have taught me a very great deal about how, and how not, to begin a new pastorate. It is my conviction that finding a good mentor is essential to a good beginning in a new pastorate, no matter how experienced the pastor or what size the congregation served. My prayer is that I have been such to those with whom I have worked.

My love and far-beyond-words gratitude go to my beloved family — my wife Pat, my son Jordan, my daughter Rachel — for their graceful incarnating of God's love again and again and again.

Introduction

How one starts a ministry in a new setting sets the tone for how that ministry will unfold for years to come. Lackadaisical, casual beginnings that mostly repeat what has worked elsewhere often lead to years of drifting and unfocused ministry. On the other hand, high energy, overdrive beginnings often lead to burned-out pastors who soon leave, thinking a move to yet another field of service is their only hope of establishing a ministry of reasonable demands and expectations. Too many programmatic changes introduced too quickly in the first few months can lead to congregational resistance and backlash. Too few changes in the early going may mean the opportunity for real change passes, not to return again until the next new pastor arrives.

The challenges before and demands upon a pastor new to a congregation are usually nothing short of enormous — establishing relationships with many new people, learning new routines and traditions of a congregation, establishing oneself in the larger community — even when the new congregation is reasonably healthy. If there has been significant conflict or if the congregation has stagnated, the task is even more complex.

Having been a new pastor three times and having mentored several other pastors new to a position has led me to identify ten essential elements that make for a good start in a new ministry. These "Ten Commandments" are intended to help new ministers begin well so that their ministry may flourish and be fulfilling, both to them and to the congregations with whom they serve. And knowing how precious time can be in a new pastorate, I have endeavored to keep this book short enough that a new pastor might actually be able to read it!

Clarence Jordan, founder of the Koinonia Farms Community in Georgia, once observed that the biblical Ten Commandments are like natural law in that we cannot break them. When we do violate them, it is we who are broken, and we serve only as illustrations of the commandments' wisdom and truth. These commandments for new pastors are not like natural law. They can, and most likely will, be broken by every new pastor, to a greater or lesser extent. Blessedly, we are forgiven our mistakes, both by God and usually by the congregations with whom we are in ministry, in order that we might learn from them.

A pastor friend of mine says there is really only one commandment for the new pastor: Don't let the urgent crowd out the important! While I agree with the truth of that injunction, it is my belief that pastors who attend to the ten commandments I have set forth will have an easier and more faithful beginning with a new congregation, a beginning that sets a good and strong foundation for years of fruitful work. Avoiding some of the more common pitfalls of a new pastorate will allow new pastors' gifts to be freely and joyously offered to the glory of God and for the nourishment of Christ's church.

Thou Shalt Be a Cultural Historian

"Some Israelites have come here to search out the land."

JOSHUA 2:2

"Well, Reverend Farris, it's like this. I never saw Reverend Flint but what he had on a three-piece suit — tie, vest, wingtips, everything. Heck, in this town, even the bankers and undertakers don't wear three-piece suits! Reverend Flint just didn't get it. He never, ever took the time to get to know who we are and how we live. And that's why he's gone!"

That comment, made to me by a member of the Reverend Flint's congregation shortly after his failed ministry had come to a ragged end, points to at least two truths about new ministries. First, it suggests that congregations, like the communities of which they are a part, are cultures. All congregations have unique histories, unwritten rules, carefully observed customs, cherished traditions, spoken and unspoken expectations of ministers and members, functional norms, famous and infamous characters, powerful legends, set patterns of relating to insiders and outsiders as well as buildings and geographical settings.

And second, new ministers, like the Israelites heading into Canaan after a sojourn in another and different context, are entering a land which is new to them and must be thoroughly searched out.

Mark was a second-career minister who had grown up in a large, active, and affluent metropolitan church. However, after seminary, he found himself called to serve an established church in a rural community. In short, he found himself in a setting radically different from that which he had previously experienced. Regrettably, his model of ministry was limited to that appropriate to his large, urban church — lots of community-focused ministries, extensive education and music programs, highly liturgical worship. From day one of his work in a very different context, Mark set about the task of re-creating that small town church in the image of his previous church experience. Needless to say, the congregation, which had been in that community for over one hundred fifty years, and had seen many a pastor come and go, did not respond positively. Conflict ensued, and Mark's efforts were frustrated at every turn. Attendance at worship and church school declined sharply, giving decreased significantly, and participation in fellowship activities dried up. Finally, and wisely, since he would not adapt to his new circumstances, Pastor Mark moved to a church in an urban setting better suited to his model of ministry. But the church and its people had suffered, suffered over two years of mostly unnecessary and unproductive conflict, and suffered the humiliation of not being known and appreciated for who they were.

Like the first of the biblical Ten Commandments, this first commandment for new ministers is the most important. If the new minister gets it right and follows it well, many of the other commandments will, if they do not fall completely into place, at least pose many fewer problems. Before we can minister faithfully and effectively in a new setting, we must understand that setting in all its richness and complexity. In entering the life of a congregation, we are crossing the River Jordan. We are entering new and unfamiliar territory, and we need to search it out carefully and understand it well if we are not only to survive, but thrive, therein. And so, we need ways to unearth the details and nuances of the current culture, the history of the people, and the specifics of the place to which God has called us to serve. There are a number of ways historical-cultural explorations can be undertaken, and some of this work can be done even before the new pastor arrives on the scene.

Written Histories

Reading church and community histories, if they are available, is an obvious first step and can be quite helpful. While generally written with a positive spin, these documents can help identify important people and key turning points in the congregation's and the community's life. A close, between-the-lines reading of these, along with annual reports and governing board records (not all of them, but a sampling of those from critical times in the congregation's life) will allow the new pastor to begin to understand some of the deeper currents which have shaped the congregation. Who were the founders, and why did they form the church? How did the congregation respond after its building burned or when a major industry left the community or when there was a dramatic increase or decrease in population? What ministers are remembered fondly, and what were they like? What needs prompted new construction or remodeling? Was there a period of "glory days" that strongly imprinted the congregation's self-understanding? Are there long-standing Sunday school classes or fellowship groups that perhaps wield as much influence in the congregation's life as the governing board? What was part of the congregation's life at one point, but is no longer — a local ministry or a style of worship service, for example? When is the congregation at its best? What conflicts has the congregation engaged, and how has it handled them? Is the congregation relatively unified in its theological stance, or is there significant diversity of perspectives? What other churches are in the community, and what are relationships with them like?

By doing such reading, I learned one congregation I served had, in its earliest days, taken a special offering for the poor of its community every time the Lord's Supper was celebrated. In that act of faithfulness to Christ's command to care for the least was born the congregation's deep and abiding commitment to extend itself generously on behalf of the disenfranchised. In another, a long defunct but well-remembered "folk service" of the 1960s became the basis for continuing openness to innovations in worship. In yet another, the arrival of a new industry had meant a dramatic increase in the community's population, and a church previously stable in membership had struggled to integrate many newcomers.

Listening to the Old Timers

While written histories usually cast the past in its most favorable light and tend to soft-pedal problems, they nevertheless can give a broad overview from which to proceed to more personal and interactive cultural explorations. While much of this will happen naturally in the course of conversation, it is helpful to structure some occasions for information gathering. One I have found most helpful is to gather a few of the congregation's long-standing members in the church sanctuary to ask them to reminisce about important moments they recall happening in that special and sacred space. Weddings, baptisms, funerals, comedic moments, even the occasional memorable sermon may all be recounted. The conversation flowing among those older and faithful members is often a pleasure for the new pastor to overhear, and can be the source of crucial insight into congregational culture and dynamics.

On one such occasion, a very elderly gentleman said to the others gathered, "Remember when there was a movie projection booth up there on the back wall? And how we'd hang a sheet across the front of the chancel and show movies for the whole town?" (That, not surprisingly, occurred in a congregation with a tradition of opening its facilities, usually at no charge, for many outside groups as part of its ministry.) A gracious and rather quiet woman spoke up, — "Oh, and remember when we had that ten-inch downpour? The water just gushed through the roof. Wasn't it then that we changed to a center aisle and angled the pews towards one another so we can see each other as we worship. I like that."

— "And thank goodness for Mrs. Hasting's bequest that helped us recover from that flood! What a wonderful Christian woman she was. I still miss her." And in but a few moments, the new pastor knew where the congregation learned to keep their facilities in good repair, how the sanctuary found its present configuration, who one of the heroines of the past was, and that the congregation could see a crisis as an opportunity for change.

— "And remember when Reverend Anderson preached that sermon damning the board from here to eternity — mostly because it wouldn't go along with him — and then stormed down the aisle taking those families with him? I always thought those folks would come back, but they never did." In the long silence that followed, the sorrow over such divisiveness was palpable.

But more than just sharing and learning history, such conversation shows that the new minister cares about where the congregation has been before she arrived, and that she values the memories of the old timers. Furthermore, holding such a conversation in the sanctuary gently reminds the participants that worship is the heart of the church's life. A tour of the entire building and grounds might well follow with more memories evoked and shared. Of particular interest here is how the use of various spaces has changed over time and why. If the church has a preschool, how were its rooms used previously? If the kitchen has been moved, when and for what purpose? What prompted additions or remodeling projects?

At the end of the tour, I like to sit the group down with a cup of coffee and ask them, "And where do you think our congregation needs to go in the future?" All kinds of answers usually come forth:

— "I hope we always have our good music in worship. That's been such a blessing to me."

— "We've got to figure out how we're going to get more parking if we're going to grow."

— "We need to keep training people in caring for one another to keep our family feel, especially for folks who are new."

— "Do you think we could ever build a retirement facility? Our community really needs one."

By the end of this conversation, the members of this group know they are valued by the new pastor not only for their memories, but also for their dreams. It is likely that they will spread the word that the new pastor is eager to learn about the congregation, leading more folks to come forward with memories, stories, hopes, and visions. And the new pastor will know a tremendous amount about the congregation's culture, history, and possibilities for the future.

History-Telling Congregational Supper

Another helpful approach to learning the culture is to have a congregational history-telling event in conjunction with a church supper. A good way to do this is to have people seated for the meal according to their presence during various pastorates (i.e., those who want to remember Pastor A's time at one table, Pastor B's at another, and so on, going back as far as possible). As people eat, they are asked to share what some of the congregational accomplishments were during that pastorate, and to recall what some of the challenges were. Using the word "challenges" for the second part of this exercise elicits more complete and helpful input than using the words "problems" or "failures." A designated recorder for each group takes notes on what is shared.

After the supper, all the groups are gathered. A person other than the new pastor (a colleague from another church of the same denomination is often a good choice) asks each group to share its collections of accomplishments and challenges, allowing the new pastor to be in the role of observer. These are recorded on large sheets of paper, one for each pastorate, for all to see. This is best done chronologically, from the most distant up to the most recent pastorate.

Through this activity, congregational members will learn an enormous amount about their own history and thereby become clearer about the congregation's identity. Newcomers present (and they should be particularly encouraged to attend) will be helped as they become acquainted with the congregation's journey before they themselves came to be members. Usually there is lots of laughter; sometimes more than a few tears. The new pastor gets to observe not only all the information collected on the sheets of paper, but also the congregation at work on this task. What's the mood? Who seems to dominate, and who is *not* talking (these may be crucial people to listen to at another time)? Where are the awkward silences when something important, and perhaps painful, may not be coming out in full? And what are the main themes, traditions, commitments over time that distinguish this congregation's life? These issues will become clearer through this evening of reminiscing and storytelling, and with them much of the congregational history and culture. The pastor's later review of the sheets will help continuities and norms of the congregation's life begin to emerge so that a sense of the parameters within which the congregation functions can be discerned.

Much more detailed and structured approaches for analyzing congregational culture are available, and it may be useful for the new minister to draw upon these, particularly if the congregation has recently, or repeatedly, experienced significant conflict. The roots of church conflict often run deep into its history, and the careful searching out of the background and sources of conflict will be essential in getting off to a good start.

It will also be worth the new pastor's time to contact one or more of the previous pastors of the congregation, particularly those pastors who served during a time of significant change in the church's life. The same issues of achievements and concerns explored by the congregation can be addressed fairly briefly, but often from a different, and hopefully insightful, perspective. Furthermore, make sure to check in with either a leader (i.e., bishop or executive) or long-term member of the denomination's regional governing body to get his or her perspective on what have been the identifying marks and moments of the congregation's life. Simply asking, "What comes to mind when you think of First Church?" will give a helpful capsule view of the congregation.

The Larger Community

Such historical and cultural explorations should not be limited to the congregation itself, as if the congregation lived in a vacuum apart from its community context. Understanding the community, and how it and the church interact, is crucial. An easy and usually pleasant way to learn about the community is to take an old timer (rather than a Chamber of Commerce community booster), either from within or without the church, and drive all over the community in which the church is located. This may take some time, especially if the church is in a large urban area, but it is time well spent. Asking the tour guide questions about how neighborhoods have changed, who lives in what neighborhoods, what abandoned buildings used to house, what used to be where new housing is going up, where people came from who lived in the community (e.g., ethnic migrations), what the economic base is and how it has changed over the years, what the schools are like, and so forth will yield an abundance of information. A good tour guide will share anecdotes that will help the new pastor begin to understand the local language, historical references, and legendary characters.

On such tours in different communities, I have quickly learned about the town dairy which had stood where the new high school now was located; about how and when the Italian American community had come to town, primarily to work as stonemasons; about past neighborhood rivalries so strong that crossing the wrong bridge into the wrong neighborhood could lead the offender to an unintended swim in the river below; about how the many churches in a city came to exist; about the environmental commitments of a developer who had beautifully laid out several subdivisions; about what a now-abandoned factory had meant to a community and what happened when the business had closed; about where to buy the freshest and cheapest seafood; about where the poor had moved when displaced by gentrification; and about a local eccentric who sometimes got into a car stopped at a traffic light and asked to be taken home.

As the community tour is taken (and on other occasions), it is helpful for the new pastor to ask people she meets who are not members of the church what their impression of the church is. Is it perceived as friendly or unfriendly? Does it have a special program like a Christmas pageant or Lenten music presentation or Vacation Bible School that is valued by the larger community? Is it known as a church willing to help people in need? Listen to discern if there are significant differences between the church's self-perception and that of the larger community.

"Café Society"

In every community, no matter whether urban, suburban, small town, or rural, there are "local watering holes" where much of the community interaction occurs. Whether cafés or coffee shops, lunch counters or fast-food restaurants, pizza joints or taverns, time spent listening carefully in these gathering places will yield a wealth of information about how the community functions. It may take a while before the regulars begin talking freely, but the wise minister who lingers over a cup of coffee will eventually learn how the community sees the church being served, how local politics really work, what the most crucial issues affecting the community are (e.g., schools, employment, etc.). In addition, the minister will learn the best place to get a car repaired, who's the gentlest dentist, and all manner of other helpful information!

OBEYING THIS FIRST commandment allows the new minister to begin to see how he is going to fit in. To the extent allowed by our personal identity and integrity, we can conform our behavior to that of the congregation and community where we are called to serve, and not end up being the only person in town in a three-piece suit. The church is a community shaped by the grand narrative of God's work, by its specific corporate narrative, and by the narratives of its members. People appreciate having their stories, their place, their families, and their traditions taken seriously. They know they matter when the new pastor is not so driven by his own agenda that he will not take the time to "know who we are." And they will be more open to change if they are first assured the new minister understands the nature of what he desires to change and that he is not under the illusion that all really important ministry will occur subsequent to his arrival. A new minister who is full of ideas for the new congregation and does not obey this first commandment will sooner or later meet significant congregational resistance. On the other hand, one who is not driven by any particular agenda for change and does not obey this commandment may well find a ministry beset with stagnation. We simply cannot minister to or with a congregation until we know its people and their cultural context. Beginning this task of learning the history and culture is a crucial first step, and an important ongoing work to undergird a new ministry.

As the salesmen sang in *The Music Man:* "Ya gotta know the territory!"

Thou Shalt Spend Thy Blue-Chips-for-Change on Changes That Matter

*Jesus said, "Woe to you, scribes and Pharisees,
hypocrites! For you tithe mint, dill, and cumin,
and have neglected the weightier matters of the
law: justice and mercy and faith."*

MATTHEW 23:23

In the beginning of a new pastorate, there exists a window
of opportunity for change during the so-called "honeymoon" period of the first twelve to eighteen months. During this time, the congregation is discovering who the new
pastor is, and is often more willing than at later times to
let the pastor initiate changes, even some quite substantial
ones, in the life and ministry of the congregation. A new
pastor has a certain number of significant changes she can
initiate. These are her "blue chips," and they need to be
spent wisely and well, for they are usually only two or
three in number.

· II ·

Limits to Change

One of the pastor's roles is that of change agent. Part of our calling as parish ministers is to understand a congregational culture, and then to seek to move that culture towards greater faithfulness through the thoughtful and creative blending of our own gifts and talents with those of the congregation. Cultures change slowly, and there are limits on how much change any culture can absorb in a given time period. But change they can. Indeed, a pastor friend of mine says it is time to move to a new congregation when we have moved the congregational culture in which we now labor as far as we can towards God's kingdom.

A conservative pastor came to a new parish, succeeding a pastor deemed far too liberal by the congregation. The new pastor immediately made a number of significant changes — instituted year-round Sunday school where previously it had run only from September through May; changed the Sunday morning schedule by adding a second service; published strict guidelines about whom he would and would not marry (those living together need not apply); and redirected much of the benevolence giving away from local, social action ministries and towards large, national Christian groups. These decisive actions were welcomed and applauded by the congregation. Indeed, the changes were widely seen as an appropriate and godly antidote to the undesirable style and theological position of the previous pastor.

The new pastor read the congregation's response to his initiatives as affirming whatever changes he might wish to make. He decided, somewhat ironically in light of both his conservatism and that of the congregation, that this was a church that simply loved change. And so he instituted more and more changes — redecorating projects; increased staffing; new hymnals; and bringing new members quickly into positions of leadership. And he was gone from that congregation in short order. The congregation, even though it agreed with his theology, rebelled against his excessively change-oriented leadership. He had tried to shift the congregational culture too much, too quickly, and with too little understanding. He was forced out not because of theological differences — indeed there were none — but because of his misreading of the congregation's ability to accommodate change.

Liberal pastors may also fall prey to this temptation to believe congregational cultures can absorb lots of change quickly. A faltering congregation in a medium-sized city, and newly led by such a pastor, recommitted itself to the neighborhood in which it was located, developing outreach programs to feed and clothe the homeless, underemployed, and disadvantaged of its community. It was no small feat for the church, but it made this change in its life prayerfully, thoughtfully, and well. And it experienced remarkable invigoration. The pastor, like her conservative counterpart in the preceding example, misread this cultural shift to mean that the congregation would be open to more, and more radical, programs of advocacy and empowerment for oppressed groups. And these she tried to establish. Members coming to church for Bible study found meeting rooms occupied by all manner of community groups; offices housed advocacy groups; the halls were full of children there for tutoring or recreation programs.

The congregation said, in word and deed, "No!" They didn't disagree with the need, but they simply could not accept any more change at that time in who they were as a congregation. And soon the pastor left, discouraged and frustrated, and feeling the congregation had failed to follow through on its calling when, in truth, she had misread the congregational culture.

Congregations can only manage a few significant changes at a time. And so, how the initial opportunity for change is used is a matter requiring considerable skill at discernment. Each new pastor has only a few blue-chips-for-change to spend, and they must be used wisely if they are to move the congregation's culture in a faithful, healthy, life-giving direction. This second commandment simply means new pastors must make only a few changes, and these must be changes that matter.

A pastor friend smiles and laughs to tell how he eliminated the singing of "Amen" at the end of hymns shortly after his arrival at a new congregation. He made clear his dislike of the funereal intoning of the word, particularly at the close of a rousing hymn. The congregation went along with the change with little objection. But the Sunday after he left for a new position, after nine years of non-amen-singing ministry, the congregation reinstated the singing of the dreaded word. Our few blue chips need to be spent on changes that might make a difference to the kingdom of God.

Effective Changes

If we have heeded the first commandment and have learned the nature of the congregation's culture, and if we are careful not to misread the acceptance of changes we institute, we can identify changes that will deepen and en-hance the congregation's life and ministry. Pastor Lois was called to a new parish just as the congregation was com-pleting an extensive remodeling of its Sunday school facil-ities. New carpeting, new lighting, new tables and chairs all made for a much-enhanced learning environment. All seemed well and good, she thought, except that there were persistent rumblings of discontent about remodeling rooms in an effort to revive a declining church school while the old and beautiful sanctuary was showing its age through neglect, both inside and out, both cosmetically and structurally. Furthermore, financial giving seemed to be stagnating due in part, it appeared, to resentment over this neglect.

Lois chose to spend a blue-chip-for-change on this is-sue, and raised it with the church's governing board. Doing so brought the concern for sanctuary maintenance out into the open, and released a flood of energy, followed by money, to do the long-overdue repairs. The board lis-tened to congregational concerns, prioritized needed re-pairs, and set a schedule for the various upgrades. This set a precedent for much more faithful stewardship of the congregation's facilities, and eventually allowed Pastor Lois to lead the congregation into strengthened steward-ship in support of mission work beyond the now well-maintained walls.

When I came to my most recent church, much discus-sion had already occurred about whether or not to go to a single Sunday morning worship service after many years of having two. The first service was small in attendance, was held during the Christian education hour, and was led without the presence of the church's fine choirs. The second service was large in attendance and was much enhanced musically. The governing board agonized over the decision, not wanting to hurt the feelings of those who liked the timing and intimacy of the small early service. But it was also concerned that we were becoming two congregations in a building with a sanctuary large enough to hold everyone.

Because I sensed from my congregational culture explorations a desire for more adult education on Sunday mornings, because I wanted to be able to take my turn teaching both adults and youth during the education hour (which would be impossible if I were leading two services), and because I sensed a longing among many members to be a single group at worship in order to strengthen our shared life, I decided to spend a blue chip and voiced my strong desire to go to a single service. The spending of this blue chip led the board to go that route, but they also changed the Sunday morning schedule so that we would be done by 11:30 a.m. This, it was correctly thought, would be welcomed by those who liked attending the early service so they could get on with the rest of their day after worship. The adult education program developed well, and a stronger sense of community emerged surprisingly quickly as we gathered as one church family at one service. The change proved to be the right one and was received with virtually no objection. Said one former early service attendee, "Well, I knew it wouldn't last forever, a service for just the twenty of us. And now I am glad it didn't."

On the other hand, it had long been my custom to celebrate Holy Communion as part of worship on Christmas Eve, but this had never been the practice of the congregation. I asked the governing board to add the sacrament to their cherished and hugely attended Christmas Eve service. That service concluded joyously at midnight, was filled with outstanding music, and was the only late Christmas Eve service in the community. Large numbers of people from outside the congregation attended. In addition, it was a time of homecoming for many of the congregation's college students who were delighted to see each other and the congregation at the service. The board was reluctant to change anything about the service. It was a cherished tradition. And besides, they said, serving Holy Communion would be too cumbersome with the sanctuary filled to overflowing. Nevertheless, I went ahead and spent a blue-chip-for-change and persevered in pursuing my request. In the course of the next several board meetings, I offered a variety of theological and liturgical reasons why adding the sacrament on Christmas Eve was a wise and correct action to take. At last, members of the board reluctantly agreed.

And they had been right, and I wrong. The service became confusing to the many folks from beyond the congregation, and disappointing to the many who had come home longing for something familiar and wonderful. As the board reviewed the service, one member said she understood my reasons for wanting to celebrate the Lord's Supper, but with so many nonmembers present, it really was not our church family gathering at the Lord's Table. It was clear to me I had wasted a blue-chip-for-change by being so determined in imposing my agenda on the board. And the next Christmas Eve, we returned with great joy to the familiar and beloved service. Contrary to popular wisdom, there are times to fix something that is not broken for the purpose of new possibilities of faithfulness, but this was not one of them.

Pastor Jerry came to a small and smoothly functioning congregation housed in a large building in an urban neighborhood where employment opportunities had been dwindling for some years and social services were eroding. Shortly after his arrival, a satellite clinic of one of the city's hospitals, situated in the church's neighborhood, closed for budgetary reasons. The clinic had been an important center for health services — immunizations, prenatal care, well-baby programs, various routine medical concerns like colds, and referrals for more serious medical needs. Jerry was comfortable interfacing with large organizations like hospitals, and his congregation felt called to try to respond to this neighborhood loss. Jerry and representatives of a congregational task force created to address the need approached the hospital about the possibility of reestablishing the clinic within their building at no cost to the hospital for use of the space.

The hospital realized that many of the clinic's former clients might well start appearing at its emergency room for routine care, which would be inefficient and costly. Over several months, a plan was developed to use the church space with the hospital donating excess medical equipment, physicians donating samples of commonly prescribed medications, and hospital personnel (primarily nurse practitioners) staffing the clinic at specified times. This allowed the clinic to resume many of its former functions while also serving to reduce unnecessary emergency room visits. In addition to space, the congregation provided volunteers to do clerical work and to visit with patients. The work required of the congregation was substantial, but as a focused, community-based ministry, it provided new energy and a sense of value.

Jerry had spent a blue-chip-for-change extremely wisely and in a way that brought new life to the church and its surrounding community. Somewhat unexpectedly, several new members, both from the community and from the hospital staff, joined the church because of their involvement with the clinic. Several years later, the clinic continues to function well, and the congregation is beginning to ask if there are other neighborhood needs to which they could offer their gifts, experience, and excess space in their building.

BLUE CHIPS NEED to be spent on changes that matter, and not solely to accommodate the preferences of the new pastor, no matter how soundly and theologically grounded those preferences might be. A careful discernment of the congregation's culture will identify changes that will strengthen the congregation and its ministry while allowing the particular gifts of the new pastor to be exercised. The more such changes are grounded in the congregation's cherished traditions and shared dreams, the more successful they will be. Whether such changes are an additional worship service in contemporary style, a significant building improvement, a new beyond-the-church-walls ministry, or a major revamping of the committee structure, they need to be worth the cost of change. Such changes, hopefully, will enliven the congregation and move it just a bit more toward being what God longs for it to be.

And finally, congregations need to be allowed to live with valuable, blue chip changes for a considerable period before other significant changes are contemplated or introduced. It takes time for substantive changes to sink in deeply enough to become a genuine, integrated part of the congregation's culture. Once they have become so integrated, then, and only then, can further changes be contemplated.

Thou Shalt Attend to Thy Preaching

*I became the church's servant according to God's
commission that was given to me for you, to
make the word of God fully known, the mystery
that has been hidden through the ages . . . but
has now been revealed to the saints.*

COLOSSIANS 1:25-26

At gatherings of ministers, loud lamentations are sometimes voiced over the fact that ministers, new and old, all
wear too many hats as they serve in all too many roles.
Ministers are preachers, teachers, counselors, spiritual di-
rectors, prophets, administrators, doers of justice, advo-
cates, process facilitators, leaders of worship, sacramental
officiants, visionaries, denominational committee members, meeting moderators, pastoral visitors, financial man-
agers, participants in all manner of community activities,
and are sometimes understandably seen as the chief executive officer of the local church. Amidst all these competing
claims upon pastors (to some of which the pastor may feel
ill-equipped to respond), the proclamation of the gospel
may move further and further down the pastor's priority

list. This third commandment reminds us that this must not be so. Attending to the crucial importance of preaching has benefits not only for the congregation, but for the new pastor as well.

The Importance of Preaching

Not only is preaching the way the new pastor (indeed all pastors) touches the most people at one time with the message of God's grace and justice and compassion, it is the unique and distinctive function of the pastor. If the church came to a time of severe crisis wherein one activity after another had to be curtailed, the last activity surrendered would be Sunday morning worship, and with it, preaching. When a church burns down, the first question asked is, "Where will we worship come Sunday?" This bespeaks the central importance the church bestows on worship and preaching. If we believe with Paul that "faith comes by hearing" (Romans 10:17), then we, the speakers of that faith, must give high priority to our time in the pulpit. And finally, most congregants will form their first impressions of a new pastor based upon her work as a preacher (this is true even if one is an associate pastor and does not preach often), so it is helpful to other aspects of a pastor's ministry to preach and lead worship well. Many church members will assume that if she does a good job leading worship, she will probably also do other ministerial tasks well. Conversely, if worship is led poorly, folks will start to wonder what, if anything, this minister does well.

And yet, the temptation will be to let other demands of our work take precedence. Perhaps it is always the way of evil to distract us from what we most essentially need to do, and this is certainly true of preaching. However, no one else in the church has the privilege of speaking God's particular word to people known and loved. Television preachers may be wizards of technology and (melo)drama, deft pullers of the heart strings and purse strings, but it is preachers on the front line of parish ministry who speak personally, knowing and caring for their listeners, whose words are shaped by both the needs of the people and the claim of the biblical text. Our culture is awash in sentimental religion and misconceptions of biblical teaching, and if congregational pastors do not counter these by leading the people from the pulpit into the depths of life with the living God, the people will be left with nothing more, and nothing more useless.

Preaching is a unique privilege not only in terms of God's call to the ministry of proclamation, but also in terms of the pastor's developing and ongoing relationship with the congregation. The new pastor has been called by a congregation that is implicitly, if not explicitly, affirming, "You have the gifts we need to have God's word proclaimed to us. And we want you to do it well."

New pastors may be tempted to reach into the "sermon barrel" to draw out old sermons in the early weeks and months of a new pastorate in an effort to free up time for other, seemingly more pressing, tasks. This is dangerous because the old sermons are not closely grounded in the lives of the present hearers, and that is precisely what they need and deserve. The sermon barrel's main function is as a repository for newly preached sermons, and it is to be dug into only in the direst of emergencies, never as a convenient time saver. A new pastor's early sermons need to be grounded in the here and now of his life with the congregation so it will know it is the recipient of the preacher's best effort rather than a sermon recycled from another place, time, and congregation. The question, "What is God's word to these people in this place today?" must shape the new pastor's pulpit work.

Congregations often do not realize how much time is required for sermons to be prepared and delivered well. And if the preacher is not getting as much affirmation as desired for his preaching in the early going (most congregations, after all, know every preacher is good for at least one decent sermon, and will wait until they have heard several before rendering judgment), the temptation to invest the time needed for adequate sermon development in other tasks will be great. The pressures of time, particularly in the midst of learning the culture of the new congregation, are very real. "Where do I find the time for adequate sermon preparation?" a new pastor asked in despair. "In addition to the congregation, I have a husband and children adjusting to our new setting!"

A new pastor can carve out the needed time for sermon work virtually from the moment of arrival on the field by informing the congregation of what time has been specifically set aside for sermon study and writing. Letting people know that the oft-used rubric of one hour of preparation for each minute in the pulpit is a truth, and not merely an ideal, will create a respect for that special, even sacred, time. This can be done by publicizing a clear work schedule (e.g., mornings in the office, two afternoons calling, three afternoons sermon preparation) and asking that people strictly limit their disruption of sermon preparation time to emergencies. If secretarial help is available to the new pastor, the secretary can help in protecting sermon time by naming it for callers and taking messages. This clear commitment on the new pastor's part lets the congregation know how much the pastor values his role as preacher and will increase the congregation's valuing of it as well.

Not only the act of preaching, but all of worship leadership deserves a new pastor's devout attention. The reading of Scripture, the offering of prayers, and the celebrating of the sacraments all offer the opportunity to speak and enact the gospel before and with a congregation. The new pastor will do well to set up his sermons with good (i.e., well-practiced) oral interpretation of the Scriptures, so that there is a sense of newness and expectancy created for the hearers. Anybody can read Scripture aloud, but few do it in such a way as to create anticipation of what word of the Lord will be delivered through exposition of the text. Prayers that intersect the life of the congregation with a measure of immediacy and a vividness of language may well touch those for whom a particular Sunday's sermon was not terribly germane. Taking the newly baptized, whether infants or children or youth or adults, out into the congregation will help the congregation embrace both the new members and their own role as nurturers in faith. Coming to the Lord's Table with the congregation's deepest longings offered as part of the liturgy deepens the corporate sense of our dependence on God's grace. A casual approach (e.g., fumbling with the order of worship, use of clichéd or generic prayers) by the new pastor will result in the congregation sensing something is missing, that perhaps worship is not all that important after all, that a "good enough" approach to the Creator of all is sufficient. What is missing is the pastor's diligent work in preparing for the most central act of the Christian community.

Resources for Preaching

The plethora of sermon aids, in print and on the Internet, particularly those coordinated with the widely used lectionaries, make great the temptation to use them for shortcuts in sermon preparation. Some of these aids are good and helpful; some of them are little more than shallow collections of allegedly relevant anecdotes; some of them are full-blown sermons waiting to be lifted in their entirety. I recently heard of two churches in the same city on the same Sunday having the same sermon title on their advertising boards in front of the churches, a title that could be found in a lectionary-based sermon aid for those who knew where to look! And there is more than a little evidence of creeping plagiarism when pastors tell stories lifted from such aids in the first person, as if the story actually happened to them. Preachers who appropriate others' material as if it is their own are not spending enough time contemplating the work of God in their own lives.

If there were to be an addendum to this commandment, it would be this: Read, read, read! Read good fiction, read a good daily newspaper, read biographies, read social commentary, read demanding biblical and theological studies that will sustain the exegetical and critical thinking skills learned in seminary. One of the best preachers I know says he reads forty pages of fiction each night before he falls asleep, no matter how tired he is.

"You'd be surprised how many books you can get through that way." Good reading keeps preaching rooted in "experience close to the pulse" as the poet Theodore Roethke put it, close to what matters in the depths of human life and in the greater world of which we are a part. In addition to reading, go to the theater and the movies, not only to see how other artists (for preaching is an art, make no mistake) are wrestling with great issues, but also to be conversant with what the congregation is ingesting. A congregation counts on its preacher not to be just one more rootless opinion giver, of which there are so many in our time, but rather the giver of deep, biblical reflection that will help them live faithfully in a world of immense complexity.

Preaching as Spiritual Discipline

Devotion to the task of proclamation benefits not only the congregation. Serious, dedicated, multifaceted sermon development becomes a profound spiritual discipline for the new pastor at a time when such is sorely needed. It becomes a time for growth in faith and understanding, a place for encounter with the Holy One in whose grace our lives and ministry are grounded, though we too easily forget. In other words, there are good personal as well as congregational reasons to be faithful to this commandment. This is particularly true for the new pastor who is confronted daily with the many clamoring demands of a new and unfamiliar context. New pastors do not just work on the preaching for their people; they do it for themselves, for their own spiritual nurture. Said John

Donne rightly, "For eighteen years I have preached to my-self, and let the congregation overhear." Preaching preparation is not a work for which there is never enough time. It is a central spiritual discipline of the pastor. It is time with God that nourishes the pastor for all the other claims parish ministry brings.

PEOPLE IN CONTEMPORARY culture can find any number of places other than church in which to meet their relational needs — service clubs, bowling and golf leagues, neighborhood associations. They have a multitude of educational options — community college classes, book study groups, courses over the Internet. They have no shortage of places to volunteer their time and gifts to make the world show forth a bit more of the kingdom of God. And what bookstore lacks several long shelves filled with a multitude of self-help books? What contemporary people lack is a place to gather with others before the mystery of God's self-disclosure as conveyed to them by a preacher who has accepted the task of faithful proclamation and all the demands it brings. People come to worship bringing their deepest yearnings and fears, their hopes and hope-lessness, their failings and the glimpses of the person they are in the eyes of God, all founded on the question Karl Barth said lay beneath it all, "Is it true about God?" Only the dedicated preacher can offer an answer that matters, that will empower faithful living, and that will mediate an encounter with the living God "in whom we live and move and have our being" (Acts 17:28).

The new pastor has come to a congregation that has heard someone else's wrestling with Barth's question on their behalf for some time, usually a number of years. No matter how good the previous pastor was in the pulpit, familiarity eventually dulled his ability to make himself heard. And so the new pastor is graced with an expectant congregation, a congregation longing, hoping, praying that this new voice can, as Roger Van Harn put it, be a midwife helping to give birth to God's word within and among them. Shall not this task claim the pastor's best?

Thou Shalt Be Certain the Church's Financial House Is in Order

Jesus looked up and saw rich people putting their gifts into the temple treasury; he also saw a poor widow put in two small copper coins. He said, "Truly I tell you, this poor widow has put in more than all of them; for they have contributed out of their abundance, but she out of her poverty has put in all she had to live on."

LUKE 21:1-4

The Reverend Joanna was interviewing with a pastoral search committee, and asked if the church's recently established endowment fund had in any way hurt regular weekly giving. "Absolutely not," intoned one member of the committee solemnly, obviously hoping to achieve final authority and closure on this subject. "What?" shouted another, "Our weekly receipts are down ten to fifteen percent ever since that stupid fund was set up! Nobody even knows what that fund is for!" Other members quickly joined in the argument. Joanna sat back, slightly appalled but very intrigued, to watch the vigorous and vociferous debate her question had ignited. And in a very few moments, she learned a very great deal about that congregation and its attitude toward money, much of which she had almost rather not known.

The Reverend David was called to a new position in a church with extensive and useful facilities — a large sanctuary and lovely chapel, an abundance of educational space, good office quarters, nice grounds. The congregation, however, had been dwindling in number for several years, and had been quite critical of several of David's predecessors. Furthermore, the facilities were very much in need of repair and congregational giving was inadequate to supply the needed funds. It came to light not too long after David's arrival that the church had a large endowment, of several hundred thousand dollars. Yet, David found himself stymied again and again in trying to determine exactly how much money was in the endowment, where it had come from, how it was invested, and for what purposes it might be used. His ignorance was widely shared in the congregation; only a few members seemed to know any details about the fund, and they were not talking. David began to suspect it wasn't just the gifts, or lack thereof, of his predecessors that had caused problems in the congregation, but its own habit of keeping financial secrets.

Openness about Financial Matters

Congregations are often funny about money. Where it comes from, where it goes, who gives how much, what is the place of special offerings and special funds . . . these are all questions that are best asked before a pastor begins a new position, and must certainly be answered clearly very soon thereafter. Secrecy about money in the church breeds suspicion, and suspicion hurts stewardship while undermining leadership. Appropriate confidentiality about money matters is needed: secrecy is not.

While clarity about the Christian duty to give generously in support of the life and mission of the church is needed, so is privacy concerning what each member gives. Only the person who records members' gifts should know who is giving how much, and this person needs to be well-schooled in the importance of confidentiality. A word of personal preference here: I strongly believe it is best if the person recording the gifts of the members is bonded (perhaps even a nonmember) and has been gently but unequivocally instructed by the pastor regarding privacy. Most folks want their giving to be a personal matter, and the sharing of information about who is giving how much only serves to generate gossip, envy, and resentment. What can be shared usefully is the general pattern of giving by the congregation — a chart showing how many members are giving how much per week, broken into a number of categories. This allows members to see where they fit, and can challenge them to do more, without exposing some to needless embarrassment.

And should the new minister know what everyone gives? I think not. A friend of mine who did decide to access this information was startled at what he found, particularly that some of the biggest complainers were among the stingiest givers. He felt he could never quite pastor them in the same way once he had that information. Like most of us, he just wasn't that much of a saint. On the other hand, I have known ministers who have used their knowledge of an individual's giving to exert pressure on specific people to give more. This too is inappropriate. It will enhance a new pastor's effectiveness to make clear that he will not be privy to information on anyone's giving except his own.

A place for openness about money in the church is the sharing of how much money the church has, and how it is being disbursed and invested. That is to say, any member of the congregation should be able to have accurate and easily comprehended information about total receipts and expenditures, at least once each year in an annual report, and preferably in a clear and understandable monthly financial statement. Such openness enhances both credibility and accountability.

Establishing, and living by, a church budget is part of the "wise as serpents" (Matthew 10:16) aspect of ministry. If this has not been a congregation's practice, the coming of a new pastor presents a good opportunity to make it so. This would be worth the spending of a blue-chip-for-change. Such information should include explicit information about reserves, endowments, and special funds (such as those for mission, a new organ, etc.) as well as on how actual operating expenditures compare to budgeted amounts. The very fact of this openness conveys the clear impression that no one has anything to hide. This defuses suspicion and builds congregational confidence in its leadership, including the new pastor.

There should be particular clarity about how any special funds, like endowment funds, are to be used. If only the interest is to be used, for what purposes and who decides? Under what circumstances may the principal be touched, and what is the process for doing so? Further-more, it is most helpful to have clarity on how unexpected gifts, like bequests, will be used before such a gift appears. A good policy to be instituted is for any gifts without any specifically articulated uses (i.e., "strings attached") to go into an endowment fund. Many a congregation has found that a large, unexpected gift can be almost as large a curse as a blessing. Such a gift, if no policy for its use has been put in place, can set off major congregational conflict, and such conflict has split more than one congregation. Pity the minister serving a church which gets such a gift soon after her arrival, and which has no policy for its use!

Financial Management Suggestions

It is often wise for a new pastor to ask the governing board to establish an endowment fund if one does not ex-ist. Pastor Judith came to a church without such a fund, a church that had a number of elderly members who might reasonably be expected to remember the church in their wills. In her questioning about the church's finances, she also discovered that the church had, over a number of years, borrowed several thousand dollars from its reserves in order to meet current operating expenses. These funds had never been repaid. Due to its rotating membership, the board did not fully realize that this had happened and was chagrined both at its ignorance and at having to write off the loss.

Judith asked the board to consider setting up an en-dowment fund, and to specify that only the interest from that fund would be used. Annually, half the interest gener-

ated would go to a reserve fund to meet major maintenance or facility improvement needs (e.g., a new roof or
boiler). The other half of the interest would be expended
annually on a mission project decided upon by the board.

The board responded to Judith's suggestion by saying
that in spite of the unrepaid borrowing, they saw little
need for such a fund, and that a few bequests would not in
all likelihood be large enough to amount to much. Furthermore, they were confident they could handle the use
of any unrestricted bequests that did come without caus-
ing problems in the congregation. But then, one member
said, "Remember what happened to First Church down
the street when they received that huge bequest? What a
fight! And look how many of their members came here because of that fight." Judith decided this was an issue
worth spending a blue-chip-for-change on. She pressed the
issue over several months while also allowing time for its
full exploration. Finally, the board, with a measure of re-
luctance, agreed with Judith's proposal and established
the endowment fund. Some members were quite confident
there would never be much money in that pot!

Three years later, Judith's church's endowment fund
had over two hundred fifty thousand dollars in it. Several
quite sizable gifts had been received, one specifically naming the clarity of the endowment fund's purpose and de-
sign as a motivation for the gift. Givers seemed to like the
idea that the principal of their gift would, except in the
most extraordinary of circumstances and then only with
majority vote of the congregation, remain a permanent
memorial. Many mission and maintenance projects had
been made possible by the interest generated from the invested monies. This was some humble pie the formerly re-

luctant board members did not mind eating at all. I once heard a stewardship consultant muse that it is rather remarkable how providing a well-labeled vessel to receive gifts often leads to that vessel being filled. And the key to keeping such special vessels as endowments from hurting regular giving is clarity about their nature, use, and administration.

One area of financial concern is how many churches will still let their checks be signed by only one person. This puts a lot of responsibility on one set of shoulders and, in some cases, has led to problems with accountability and even embezzlement. A much better practice, even if it is sometimes a bit cumbersome, is to have two signatures, of authorized church officers, required for every check (and neither of those signatures should be the pastor's!). Two sets of eyes reviewing, even if only briefly, each and every check drawn on the church's accounts will reduce the temptation to misuse funds.

Another financial area of concern for the new pastor has to do with how honoraria received for weddings, funerals, speaking engagements, and so forth are to be handled. Some ministers may find these a much-needed source of additional income. But if not, I have found it a helpful practice to place such funds into a "Pastor's Discretionary Fund" held by the church. These funds are money I can expend without getting anyone else's approval, although I do report both where the money came from and where it goes. The fund gives the pastor the flexibility, for example, to meet an emergency need for food or shelter or transportation quickly; or to buy flowers or a gift for a staff or church member who has rendered a special service; or to help a child go to camp whose family is not able to pay the fee.

A NEW PASTOR can help the church get its financial house in order by following the aforementioned suggestions. And that honeymoon window of opportunity for changes is an excellent time to do so. The new pastor is in an excellent position to ask for these changes, asserting simply "I would feel a lot more comfortable if we did it this way." Many others will feel more comfortable, too. Defusing suspicions about money and its use will go a long way towards raising a congregation's trust and thereby its willingness to give generously. And while St. Jerome was no doubt right in saying, "Avoid as you would the plague a clergyman with business interests," the new pastor's modeling of faithful stewardship in the management of the church financial resources will strengthen the congregation's confidence in his overall leadership ability.

• V •

Thou Shalt Not Create Expectations Which Cannot Be Met in the Long Term

Then Job answered the Lord, "I know that you can do all things, and that no purpose of yours can be thwarted."

JOB 42:1-2

Not a few ministers have the problem of being "people pleasers." Working in a profession where achievements are often not clearly seen, where work can expand to include virtually every available minute, and where interaction with others can be almost constant, can sometimes lead clergy to settle for being liked. One way to be liked is to try to emulate St. Paul's not-so-modest affirmation, "I have become all things to all people" (I Corinthians 9:22). Blessedly, we are not St. Paul, though we may be tempted by his claim. The temptation is especially strong for the new pastor who is often somewhat anxious about belonging, about fitting into his new community. We are tempted because we genuinely want to bond with people in relationships that will facilitate growth in faith, but also because we want, and need to be, accepted and valued. However, there may be a dark side to our desire to be widely approved of, and that is the unspoken hope that people who like us will do things our way and be reluctant to create conflict by disagreeing with us. But, as Job reminds us, it is God alone, and not St. Paul or ourselves, to whom the power to do all things is reserved. And we do well to remember this is so.

Creating Unrealistic Expectations

After seminary, Pastor Ben had done well in his first small congregation, excelling particularly in the area of pastoral care. One behavior his congregants most appreciated was his practice of going to the hospital and sitting with the family while a loved one underwent surgery. With his calm nature, spiritual centeredness, and comforting words, Ben instilled peace and hope in anxious family members. The time came when he was called to an exceptionally large urban church as an associate pastor. He was excited about this new call because it would allow him to spend much more of his time doing the work for which he felt most gifted — pastoral care.

Ben continued his practice of sitting with families during surgeries, and again, this was enthusiastically received. But in such a large church, where as many as three or four members might have surgery in a given week, Ben found he was spending enormous amounts of his time sitting in hospital waiting rooms. There were days he would get to one hospital before six in the morning and find himself leaving another hospital well past six in the evening. He knew he was shortchanging the other responsibilities of his position, and he was not taking adequate time off for his family or himself.

V

But people loved his work. They had never known this quantity and quality of pastoral attention. His ministry was celebrated in the conversations of church members. Soon everyone in the church who was to have surgery was resting in the sure expectation that Pastor Ben would be caring for their family while he or she was in the operating room. Ben, with the best of intentions, had created a monster. And he simply could not continue to meet this expectation. As often happens with good people, he had been tempted not through his weakness, but through his gift.

Finding a way out of this situation seemed almost hopeless. He considered leaving parish ministry and entering hospital chaplaincy, but feared that would only make matters worse. He considered going to another church and beginning by setting a very different pattern of caring for patients' families, but he and his family liked the city and neighborhood in which they had become established. Finally, he decided to begin the excruciatingly hard work of changing the congregation's expectations, which he simply could not continue to fulfill. With the support of the other pastoral staff, Ben did so by beginning to set boundaries on when and how long he would be with families. The backlash was predictable. "But you stayed with Marian's family the whole time!" Excruciatingly hard as it was at times, Ben stood his ground. At the same time, he started recruiting and training laypeople in how to be spiritual partners in waiting with families. Several church members found they were gifted for this work and were delighted to be part of this ministry of compassion. Gradually, the word spread and expectations shifted. It was not easy for Ben, and there were numerous uncomfortable, even painful, moments with parishioners. But Ben finally got balance back in his life and work. However, to the conclusion of his ministry with that congregation some years later, members with whose families Ben had sat for hours and hours early on would come up and whisper with some pride, "I'm so glad you stayed with my family."

Similarly, Reverend Sarah was a high-energy person who could not wait to get started at her new church. And she started with exuberance! She went to every meeting of every group in the congregation — board meetings, committee meetings, prayer group meetings, Bible study groups, youth fellowships, women's circles, men's breakfasts, and even sang in the choir. At first, people were surprised to see Sarah everywhere, since that had not been her predecessor's practice, and more than one church member had to bite a tongue to keep from saying, "What are you doing here?"

But as time went on, folks got used to Sarah being at everything. Soon, they took her presence for granted. And before long, they came to count on her being present. In fact, the situation went rather quickly from Sarah being at everything to nothing happening without Sarah being present. The church was in a growing community and was itself growing in numbers and activity. And so, there were more and more meetings for Sarah to attend. With the best of intentions, she had created dependency and suppressed the leadership of the very people with whom she had come to be in ministry. Of course, her family complained of her absence regularly, but Sarah felt everything at church would start to malfunction if she stopped going to all the meetings.

Not surprisingly, it was Sarah who eventually began to malfunction and burn out. She was a likable person and almost everyone was fond of her, but as her effectiveness decreased, the time came when the governing board suggested it was time for her to seek another call or take an extended leave. They cared for her, to be sure. But although it was never quite said aloud, they also wanted their church back. To her credit, Sarah left graciously and took several months off to rest herself and reconnect with her family. She entered therapy to search out the roots of her over-involvement. And eventually, Sarah returned to parish ministry renewed and freed from her well-intentioned, but self-defeating, behavior.

Setting Boundaries

Both the congregation and the pastor suffer when unrealistic expectations, often imported from another context, are created in the early stages of a new pastorate. The congregation will suffer the inevitable disappointment of unrealized expectations. And the pastor will be on the fast track to exhaustion. The remedy for this problem is to make a realistic assessment of how one's gifts may best be shared in the new context (see commandment number one), and to go slowly and clearly in setting realistic boundaries for ministry in the new setting. Harder than these two steps, and in the long run much more essential, is for the pastor to take time to do the essential work of self-examination. In particular, pastors who find themselves always on the run or always talking about how busy they are morning, noon, and night, need to stop and do the hard work of setting boundaries, both on behalf of their congregations and themselves.

The Ignatian spiritual tradition of "examen," of honest self-assessment on a regular, even daily, basis can be adapted to help in the setting of appropriate boundaries. The task itself is simple, but requires freedom from self-deception. Somewhere near the end of each day, the new pastor would do well to review the day's activities, hour by hour, asking questions such as:

- Did I need to do that activity?
- Was it the best, or at least a good, use of my gifts and time?
- Did I deny someone else the opportunity to minister by doing that activity?
- Did I do that work to honor God, or was I serving my own ego needs?
- What did I not do, particularly with my family, because of that activity?
- Am I resentful, or feeling like I have to do that work?
- Who do I feel is making me do work I don't want to do but feel I must?

This exercise is done as an act of prayer, and all of the answers are offered to God. Such an honest and prayerful act of reflection can help significantly in the never-ending task of learning to be responsible stewards of our gifts, our time, and our relationships. It can empower us to act faithfully in our other vocations as spouse, as parent, as friend, and as adult child of aging parents as well as our vocation as pastor. If some persistent failing to set realistic boundaries — which thereby creates unrealistic expectations among the congregation — keeps cropping up during this examen, the need to enter into a therapeutic relationship may well be indicated. This may take the form of either psychological counseling or spiritual direction, either individual or group, as we seek to discern the sources of our dis-ease and to find the ability to change it.

As the preceding examples from two new pastors' experiences in violating this commandment reveal, how a new pastorate is begun can set the pattern and tone for ensuing years. The new pastor needs to take care not to trap himself and to ensure that his actions are not injurious to the development and use of members' gifts for ministry. Furthermore, it is clear the new pastor can pay a crushing personal price for creating unrealistic expectations, and that the way out of such situations is rarely easy. What worked well in one parish does not necessarily automatically transfer to another (see the first commandment). New means of using our gifts need to be discerned for ministry in a new context with the new congregation. In addition, doing the work for which we as pastors are affirmed is not always best for the laity. Doing it all, and all on our own, can impede the ministry of the laity, and thereby hinder their growth as disciples who have found their own God-given gifts and the right uses of them. Observing this commandment starts both the new pastor and the congregation down a road leading to healthier, more faithful, more broadly shared ministry.

The story is told of a young associate pastor who entered the senior pastor's study one afternoon. The slumping shoulders, the downcast eyes, the flop into a chair made clear that all was not well in the associate pastor's world. After waiting for some minutes for the associate to speak, the older pastor finally asked, "What's wrong?" With a great sigh, the associate said, "I feel I have let God down." Replied the older and wiser colleague, "And who, pray tell, told you that it is your job to hold God up?"

Let those who have ears, hear.

Thou Shalt Take Care of Thyself from Day One

Jesus said, "The first commandment is
  'Hear, O Israel:
The Lord our God, the Lord is one;
You shall love the Lord your God
With all your heart, with all your soul,
With all your mind and with all your strength.'"

MARK 12:29-30

The elements of the self as Scripture understands it —
heart, soul, mind, strength — are the tools with which we
fulfill Jesus' command to love God with all that we are. If
these tools are not maintained, our capacity to love God is
diminished, no matter how good and honorable our intentions. After all, everyone knows where that paved-with-
good-intentions path leads. Yet, in the crush of the newness a pastor meets in coming to a new congregation, the
temptation to delay the time when caring for self will begin is strong. It may well seem that there are just too many
competing claims on the new pastor for her to take the
time needed for appropriate self-care. The paradox of this

situation is that it is precisely the lack of self-care that will eventually cripple her ability to meet those many demands in seeking to be faithful to Jesus' commandment.

Heart, soul, mind, and strength describe the fullness of the human being, with the heart corresponding to the emotional life, the soul to the spiritual life, the mind to the intellectual life, and strength to the physical life. While we are not all equally fit in all four dimensions, attentiveness to each of them is essential for the well-being of the whole person, the whole pastor. Usually, an individual will be strongest in one or two of these dimensions, and may be tempted to live mostly out of the strongest areas of the self. A person gifted in mind who finds it pleasant and stimulating to live in the world of ideas and language may rely too much on this dimension at the expense of the emotional or physical self. The mystic, on the other hand, who is nourished by solitude and prayer may lack sufficient physical stamina to meet the demands of a busy congregation. Seeking to find balanced development of all four dimensions will not only enhance a pastor's ability to love God, but also to love those with whom he shares ministry.

Faithfulness in the care of our selves needs to begin as soon as the new pastorate begins in order that well-defined patterns of care for each dimension are built into the pastor's schedule before other demands crowd them out. This not only models for the congregation what it means to care appropriately for the self we have each been given by the God in whose image we are made, it also clarifies expectations (see commandment five) about how the pastor's time will be spent.

Emotional Self-Care

How might we care for the heart, the emotional self? Here
the support of family and friends is crucial. If the new pastor has a family, that family must be given high priority,
not only because family members will have their own
transition issues and not only because of the obligation to
be a good spouse and parent, but also because the family
is a place where the pastor can receive love and nurture.
And the pastor must remember that his family is not a col-
lection of unpaid associate pastors! A minister I much ad-
mire once said that, at the beginning of his ministry, his
order of priorities was God, church, family. But as time
went on, the order shifted to God, family, church, and he
felt he and his family as well as the church were healthier
for the change. What he had done was to bring his vocations as spouse and parent into better balance with his
pastoral vocation and his baptismal vocation as a Christian.

Friends are also essential to our emotional well-being,
and are particularly so for the single pastor. These may
sometimes come from within the congregation, particularly if it is a larger church situated in an urban or suburban context. But many new pastors will also find it beneficial to seek friends from beyond the congregation
(particularly in smaller communities) and preferably some
who have few or no expectations of the pastor as a pastor,
who may not even be particularly impressed with that line
of work. One minister shared with me that her best friend
is an agnostic who not only was not particularly impressed she was a minister, but whose questions and conversation helped keep her honest about her own theology.

Another pastor notes how a biweekly breakfast with a friend who always asks "How are you?" rather than "How's your work?" sustains him.

The important distinction between family and friends, and the congregation, is that the former love and care for us for who we are, and not, like the latter who often tend to be more concerned to be on the receiving end of pastoral attention, for what we can do for them. Often family and friends may, like God, have to love us in spite of ourselves, especially as they see the parts of us that we try to keep hidden from our congregants as we go about our ministry — resentment, tiredness, sense of inadequacy, fear of failure. And often, the love of God is mediated to the pastor by family and friends who, like Mr. Rogers, "like us just the way we are." Scripture speaks truly, "We love because God first loved us" (I John 4:19). It is the experience of being loved and accepted as we are, and the continual renewal of that experience, that empowers our own efforts at loving. God's people, who depend on our capacity to mediate God's love to them, particularly in times of need, also depend on us to allow our capacity to love to be renewed.

One further aspect of caring for the emotional self is cultivating the ability to receive. Too many pastors are too driven by the scriptural affirmation that it is "more blessed to give than to receive" (Acts 20:35). In our drivenness to obtain that blessing for ourselves by our almost unending giving of ourselves, we may rob others of it. Receiving graciously is a blessing, too — especially for the giver. Members of a congregation will be frustrated in their efforts to know the blessing of giving if their pastor dismisses compliments or is mostly embarrassed by gifts intended to convey gratitude and appreciation. A too rigid defining of the pastor as "giver" and church members as "receivers" not only frustrates the latter; it deprives the pastor of an opportunity to be healthier emotionally.

Good relationships with colleagues are also key to the pastor's emotional well-being. Simply put, it is most helpful to be in relationships with other ministers who understand experientially the complexities and idiosyncrasies of serving as a parish pastor. "Lone Ranger" pastors end up lonely, without fail. The new pastor will do well to find a group of other colleagues with whom to meet on a regular basis. Such a group might be formed with other pastors of the same denomination who meet for food and fellowship, to share one another's joys and burdens, and for prayer. Or the group might be an ecumenical group that reads theological works or does sermon preparation work together. My experiences with both types of groups have been immensely strengthening. The denominational group provides the understanding and easy communication possible among folk who share a common perspective while the ecumenical study group has broadened my view of the Christian experience because of its denominational, gender, and age diversity. Any such group can be a blessing by virtue of holding one another in prayer at each gathering. And they may also include social gatherings like dinners and parties where good food and hearty laughter bring their own healing.

So much of ministry involves strong emotions — the joy of marriage or a new, healthy child; the pain of grief; the anxiety over aging parents or growing children. Attentiveness to the well-being of our emotional selves is essential if we are to share the emotional life of those whom we pastor.

Spiritual Self-Care

The pastor is the spiritual leader of the congregation, and nowhere is this clearer than in the leading of God's people in worship. But we deceive ourselves if we believe that we can truly and deeply worship while leading others in that activity. In those sacred moments, we are working (and usually quite hard) to create a time when church members can come freely and trustingly before God to find healing, meaning, renewal, and empowerment. The people will leave, we hope and pray, refreshed and challenged by their encounter with the living God, but the pastor usually goes home tired from a hard morning's work. Sunday morning is not often a time for our own spiritual renewal, and we will soon be in trouble if we tell ourselves otherwise. Just as we cannot love without having had the experience of being loved, so we cannot bring the water of life to others if our own spiritual well is dry.

That means we need to be intentional about finding opportunities for spiritual growth. Is there a retreat center nearby? Consider scheduling a morning or day there at least every other week. Use that time for prayer and meditation and journaling, and go especially when everything seems to be going great and there appears to be little pressing need to go. Is a spiritual director available nearby? Probably so as more and more people have developed their gifts for this ministry. Find and meet with one regularly in order to receive insight into what God is about in your life and guidance for whatever devotional practices you may follow. Is there another church nearby that offers a worship service at a time other than Sunday morning (perhaps midweek or Sunday evening)? I know ministers who take communion at a midweek service every week, and find it a great blessing to be on the receiving end of the sacrament. Recent years have brought forth an enormous amount of quality written material on spirituality. Read and savor it, perhaps with others. Opportunities abound for extended retreats, workshops, and conferences on spiritual growth and formation. Go and be fed.

Finally, I believe that space is made sacred by regular prayer. The new pastor who begins her day with a time of prayer — silent, meditative, chanting, singing, or spoken — in the sanctuary where she will lead God's people in worship will find that space gently transformed. There's a difference in space that is used only for the glorification of God, and space that is used for all manner of other human activity. That is to say, that just as sermon preparation can be an act of devotion which blesses the preacher as well as the congregation, so prayer in the sanctuary can be a gift to both pastor and congregation as it shapes towards holiness that room of rooms.

We seek to minister out of the fruit of the Spirit — "love, joy, peace, patience, kindness, generosity, faithfulness, gentleness and self-control" (Galatians 5:22). Such fruit will be found in and through us as we attend to our own spiritual health.

Intellectual Self-Care

How can we care for the mind, the intellectual self? I have already written of the importance of reading and of the arts under commandment number three. Another essential part of our caring for the mind has to do with the use of any continuing education time the congregation may extend to the new pastor. Seminaries, church institutes, and any number of independent ministries offer myriad study and growth opportunities. The value of these is found not only in the content we absorb while attending such events, but also in the relationships we form and in the simple fact of being away from our usual context with all its relentless demands. Freedom from the usual routines and expectations frees the mind for new possibilities, wonder, and growth.

If we have identified an area of self or ministry that is underdeveloped, continuing education time can be used to address that need (and to do so with a measure of anonymity, which may be desirable). I have spoken with a pastor who recommends using such time to explore subjects that may be only tangentially related to ministry. He has gone to workshops on alternative medicine, writing for publication, gardening, and home construction! Ultimately, all of these in some way augmented his ministry (he began a program to help urban residents garden on vacant lots and worked in Habitat for Humanity). Understandably, most congregations will want the pastor to justify her use of continuing education time so that they may see the benefit of it, but the pastor knows that part of the benefit is the mental stimulation that comes from exploring a new or unfamiliar area.

Creative activity is also beneficial to intellectual health. Pastor Rebecca swore she spent every ounce of her creative energy in giving birth to a sermon each week, and the fruits of her labor were clearly apparent. But then a good friend persuaded her to join a ceramics class. Rebecca ended up becoming quite a good potter. And her preaching suffered not a bit. In fact, having a whole new realm of sensation and metaphor to draw on enhanced her work as a preacher. Other creative activities to which ministers have testified in terms of mental renewal include gardening, woodworking, needlework, painting, and gourmet cooking. And there are many more. Any creative endeavor that stretches the pastor into a new and different area of expertise can renew the mind.

St. Paul knew whereof he spoke when he said, "Do not be conformed to this world, but be transformed by the renewing of your mind" (Romans 12:2).

Physical Self-Care

In what ways can we care for our strength, the physical self? Who among us is unaware of the benefits of eating properly and of exercise, and of their necessity for our long-term well-being? That gospel is so prevalent as to leave guilt-ridden those who ignore it. But it also happens to be true. So much of ministry is sedentary — sitting listening to troubled people, sitting while studying and writing, sitting doing administrative work, sitting in countless meetings, sitting in the car as we travel from one task to the next. Thank goodness we get to stand to teach and lead worship!

The care of the body is critical not only as an end in itself; it is also supportive of our emotional, spiritual, and intellectual well-being. Not that we cannot be healthy in these other dimensions of the self in the midst of illness. Quite the contrary is true. Illness of the body can certainly stimulate growth in the other dimensions. But in the normal course of life, we feel better, we focus better, we think better if our bodies are reasonably healthy and not distracting us with aches and pains. Obsession with the body is a significant problem in our culture and time, as a trip to almost any health club will make clear, but that is not the issue for most pastors. Lack of adequate exercise often, and sadly, is.

So, it is incumbent upon us to find some pulse-elevating, strength-enhancing, respiration-quickening, muscle-stretching exercise we more or less enjoy, and to do it regularly. Three times a week is good; five is better. And exercising with others can make it more pleasant, although a good many pastors may find their exercise regimen can also be a private time for prayer and meditation. "I pray a lap in the pool for each member of my family and each needy member of my congregation every time I swim," says one ministerial devotee of the natatorium. Some meditate best in the sauna after their workout, and others may pray while walking briskly. If we believe the body is a gift of God, then caring for it is an act of stewardship. Exercising regularly and eating well are not self-serving, but rather are intended to enhance our ability to offer ourselves in loving service to God and others.

And please, schedule a day off right from the beginning of a new pastorate. If you have children, you may want it to be Saturday in order to have time with them. Whatever day you choose, let it be known to the congregation. And let it be gently known that you, like every other biblical person, not only need, but are commanded to take, sabbath time. Such time is crucial to care for all the dimensions of the self. Entering a new pastorate is a good time to begin these disciplines of caring for the whole self. As time passes and routines grow and grow in their determinative power, it becomes increasingly difficult to establish patterns of appropriate self-care. A pastor who establishes such patterns early on, creating them not out of love for the self but for God, can model such helpful behaviors to parishioners, some of whom may believe that only the soul matters and therefore neglect the body, or that only what one feels matters and therefore neglect the mind. Through the pastor's caring for the whole self, as Scripture understands it, others may also be led to better self-care, which will in turn make them more useful to the kingdom of God.

FAR FROM BEING an exercise in self-indulgence, appropriate self-care for the whole person is a path of faithfulness to Christ's command and a way of honoring God in whose image we are fashioned. Jesus rejoiced in relationships, spent hours in prayer, studied Scripture deeply, exercised, and loved the pleasure of table fellowship. In following his example, we are both faithful disciples and more effective pastors.

Thou Shalt Be Aware of the Chronics

Jesus said, "If anyone will not welcome you or listen to your words, shake off the dust from your feet as you leave that house or town."

MATTHEW 10:14

"Chronic" is a word not customarily used as a noun. I use it so here to refer to those folks in almost every congregation, blessedly few in number, whose lives are seemingly dedicated to long-standing patterns of behavior that are, at best, energy draining and, at worst, destructive. Most congregations are full of wonderful people, but these chronics are also present in many churches. They come in three varieties — the chronic havers of personal problems, the chronic complainers, and the chronic workaholics. Naivete about them can lead to serious problems for both the new pastor and the congregation. An assumption that what these individuals need is the warmth and compassion they have not received from previous pastors can be more than a little damaging to the ministerial effectiveness of the new pastor.

Chronic Personal Problem Havers

This first group of chronics includes people whose energy is dedicated to having a personal problem rather than to solving it. Generally, they are among the first congregational members to seek pastoral care or counseling from the new minister. The new pastor will do well to attend closely to who comes through his study door seeking help in the first few weeks. Chronic personal problems havers are often flattering. They suggest, in subtle and not so subtle ways, that they are sure the new pastor has been sent by God to help them with their issues. The clear implication is usually that the previous pastor was not so sent or qualified. Their appeal for help may help assuage the insecurities of the new pastor by suggesting it is this pastor's giftedness that will surely help them at last. And they often use the language of faith in presenting what is troubling them.

Mitch was a likable, longtime member of the congregation to which Pastor Andrew had recently come. Mitch's problem was his mother, who lived in the same community but was not a member of the church. She was the bane of his existence, he said. She ran his life by constantly telling him what to do, and by being verbally cruel when he did not measure up to her expectations. And according to Mitch, he was such a good son. His mother was in good health but had never learned to drive, so Mitch had driven her everywhere since his father's death some years previously. Mitch's wife understandably resented this, and let him know it. Mitch stopped at his mother's home to visit her every single day, as a good son-in-the-same-city should. He called her and she called him, regularly, both at home and at work. Mitch talked openly, and to most everyone it seemed, about his overbearing mother. But what could he, as a good Christian person, do? Wasn't he commanded by Scripture to honor his mother?

What Mitch could do, of course, was to seek the new pastor's counsel. And this he did within two weeks of Andrew's arrival. Faithfully and skillfully, Andrew listened to Mitch and sought to discern the outlines of his problem. Mitch dominated most of the counseling sessions with his unending talk, and yet left each session affirming how great was the help Pastor Andrew had offered. Andrew, for his part, found it hard to keep the sessions within the allotted hour, and allowed Mitch to schedule two appointments each week since he seemed to be so earnest about wanting to deal with the issue of his mother. Between appointments, Mitch started calling Andrew at the office and at home to talk over the latest incident with his mother. He told other church members he was working with Pastor Andrew on this issue.

But whenever Andrew made suggestions of alternative ways for Mitch to interact with his mother ("Have you thought of giving her driving lessons as a Christmas present?"), Mitch always had a reason why they would not work. Even when Mitch himself came up with a new possibility, he never followed through on it. Andrew found himself wondering regularly if he were approaching Mitch's problem in an ineffectual manner.

Finally, out of his frustration, Andrew talked to a colleague about the situation. Through this consultation, he realized that Mitch had no intention of changing his relationship with his mother, and was, in fact, virtually ad-

dicted to talking about the problem rather than address-
ing it through concrete behavioral changes. Pastor
Andrew found that he had been drawn into Mitch's resistance to change. Mitch's problem with his mother was a
way of life for him. However, Andrew was concerned that
if he started limiting his contact with Mitch that Mitch
would turn on him and perhaps tarnish his reputation as a
counselor by telling others that the new pastor was, after
all, not really very helpful.

With the support of his colleague, Andrew did begin
to take appropriate control of the counseling relationship.
He began by limiting Mitch to one appointment per week,
and kept that appointment strictly to fifty minutes. He
asked his family and secretary to take messages from
Mitch rather than speaking to him directly whenever he
called. He stopped making any suggestions of changed behavior for Mitch to try.

And Mitch did indeed become critical of Andrew's
counseling — sometimes directly to Andrew, often to others in the congregation. Within six weeks, Mitch stopped
making appointments and would not accept Andrew's
suggestion of a referral to a therapeutic professional because "he wanted a Christian" to help him with his problem, and because he felt his own pastor should be that person.

Thereafter, a curious thing happened. Pastor Andrew's
secretary said in passing one day that some church members had wondered how long it would take him to catch
on to Mitch. And suddenly, Andrew realized that the
problem was not only that Mitch only wanted to talk
about, rather than act, on his problem. A much larger issue was that, because Mitch spoke freely to other mem-

bers, the congregation had been watching the whole scene and judging Andrew's pastoral effectiveness by how he handled it. In other words, the congregation was well aware of who the chronic problem havers were and was judging the new pastor's skill as a counselor in part by whether or not he could recognize this type of individual. Had Andrew continued to be ensnared in Mitch's time-devouring apathy, his ability as a counselor would have been profoundly compromised in the eyes of many members. Sometime after the counseling relationship with Mitch had concluded, Andrew found other members, mostly sincerely motivated by a desire to address their issues, approaching him for help.

Pastor Andrew was wise in seeking guidance from a colleague on this matter. He trusted his feelings of resentment towards Mitch and his fear of ineffectiveness, and these led him to seek another pastor's perspective on the situation. He also used this frustrating situation as an incentive to start finding a network of skilled counselors and effective groups to whom he could refer those he felt unable to help or with special needs best handled by experts. He visited several counselors to find out their areas of expertise and their attitudes towards people of faith. He checked out a number of self-help groups such as Alcoholics Anonymous to determine when and where they met, and when they accepted newcomers. These steps proved to be extremely helpful in his continuing work, and helped him become much more effective in his counseling ministry within the congregation.

So, be aware of the chronics as this commandment enjoins, especially this first type. Not only can they consume enormous amounts of time, they have the potential to make the pastor feel ineffective and to cause him to be seen as ineffective by others.

Chronic Complainers

The second type of chronic is the chronic complainer. These individuals speak frequently to both the pastor and to other church members about what is wrong with "this church." Rarely do they frame their complaints in terms of "my church" or "our church," but rather "this church." Perhaps they had a better church experience else-where, perhaps they are comparing "this church" with some impossible ideal of a faith community, but whatever the case, their language indicates they experience them-selves as at some distance from the congregation, that the church has not become their own in some important way.

Chronic complainers may not like the music the choir sings, the kinds of activities the youth are involved in, or the appearance of the church building and grounds. They sometimes begin their lament with "When Pastor Wonder-ful was here. . . ." The new pastor may try to avoid them, or she may try to counsel them, or she may finally explode at them. None of these approaches will do much good. These people will neither be ignored nor silenced. They usually will not respond to individual counseling because they are certain it is others, not they, who have a problem. Getting angry with them only serves to drive them into further isolation. And it is isolation, a sense of not belong-ing, that is often behind their complaining. For whatever reason — personality type, newness to the community, an old grudge or hurt — they do not experience themselves as belonging to the community of faith. It is this feeling of isolation that underlies their constant complaining.

A wise new pastor will try to get them involved in an area of the church's life where they can begin to experience meaningful relationship with other members. Often it is useful to enlist the aid of a compassionate church member to invite, and accompany, the chronic complainer to a study group, a committee meeting, or a fellowship activity. It is not prudent to involve them in, much less put them in charge of (although the temptation may be great to say, "Okay, you do it!") a group responsible for the area about which the complaints are being made. That may come later, but only after the complainer feels a part of the congregation's life and ministry. The chronic complainer's most frequent need is to belong (although there are certainly some who have significant control issues), and a new pastor often has an opportunity to help them that may have been unavailable to the previous pastor, who may have simply come to endure them as a cross to bear. Helping them find a way to belong best ministers to them, too. The truly chronic complainers may resist such help, or try it and then delight in announcing why it failed. At that point, they may have joined the group of chronics previously identified. But often, they can be gently led to becoming part of "our church."

Chronic Workaholics

In almost every congregation, there are a few individuals who seem to be involved with everything that goes on. Sometimes they are newcomers anxiously trying to find a way to fit it; more often they are old-timers who have been around forever, who know where everything is and how everything is done, and just step in to take care of matters. Newcomer workaholics are usually not problematic because they eventually calm down and narrow their focus once they have found a niche in which to offer their gifts. But the old-timers, even if well-intentioned, may be acting out of a need to control. Their over-functioning may lead to apathy or anger in others who have gifts appropriate to various tasks but are not afforded the opportunity to use them.

Veteran workaholic church members, somewhat like chronic complainers, often need to know they matter to the life of the congregation. Out of their love for God, they have often given much to the church. They need to know they and their contributions are valued so that their over-doing does not lead others to resent them. Publicly recognizing them for their many years of labor can sometimes create space for them to enjoy a bit of sabbath time at last. Finding a new area of ministry for which their wide knowledge and willingness to serve (and perhaps giving them responsibility for it while clearly indicating it is this work, and not others, where their gifts are needed) can help. And they are often among the very best people to ask to participate in history taking events such as that previously described (see commandment number one).

In the crush of tasks to be done in the beginning weeks of a new pastorate, new pastors may be particularly vulnerable to relying excessively on the chronic workaholics, and thereby reinforce the very behavior that needs changing for their sake and the sake of others. Pastors are generally, and understandably, looking for hardworking church members who do their part to invigorate congregational life. And many pastors are themselves not unfamiliar with the temptations of workaholism. It is thus of particular importance that the new pastor be clear in adhering to the biblical injunction to take sabbath time. As previously mentioned, personal sabbath time needs to be taken by the pastor as an act of self-care and as a gentle instruction to others. The importance of sabbath can be the subject of preaching as well as of written church communications such as newsletters. One pastor writes a personal letter to each board member completing a term of service in which the lay leader is encouraged, to the point of gentle admonishment, to take a year of sabbath time away from most church responsibilities, save worship, in order to rest in the Lord and to be renewed for future service. Such can be helpful measures in working with chronic workaholics.

The Chronically Ill

One other group of chronics is utterly different from the three already discussed. These are the chronically ill, particularly those whose participation in the life of the congregation is restricted by their illness. These people need and deserve the pastoral energy that is so easily siphoned off by the chronic problem havers, complainers, and workaholics. And yet, because they are often not the proverbial "squeaky wheel," the chronically ill sometimes do not receive the pastoral care they should.

A perceptive new pastor will take care to identify the chronically ill and homebound soon after her arrival at the new church and will place them at the very top of her list of pastoral calls to be made. These individuals need to be known, and they need to know they matter to the pastor and the congregation even though their activity in the church's life and work may be quite limited. Often they are older and can share wonderful and helpful memories of the church's history that will be immensely valuable to the new pastor as she goes about learning the congregation's history and culture.

A most important work in which the chronically ill can participate is the work of intercessory prayer. The act of praying for others — for a child of the church school who is their special concern, for a new ministry the church is undertaking, for the officers of the church — helps not only the prayed for, but also those who pray. It helps them feel they can still contribute to the church's life and lessens feelings of uselessness or dependency. Furthermore, the new pastor should not underestimate how the chronically ill often delight in receiving Holy Communion in their homes, particularly in the week following the congregation's celebration of the sacrament. In this act, they are not only renewed spiritually but also reminded of their valued place among the communion of saints.

Pastoral attentiveness to the chronically ill lets other church members know that they too may depend on being cared for if and when they are beset by illness. It lets them know the pastor cares not only for the doers of the church who actively carry out its ministry, but also for those too easily and often seen as the least within the church. As the pastor discerns active members who are gifted for the ministry of visitation and friendship, she can recruit and train them to develop deep and nurturing relationships with the chronically ill through visits, letters or cards, and gift exchanges. These relationships bless both persons profoundly, especially as the chronically ill are often the congregation's best teachers of how God bestows presence and strength in times of need.

Be aware of the chronics, and attend to them appropriately.

Thou Shalt Limit Thy Activities beyond the Congregation That Has Called You

Let your "Yes" be yes and your "No" be no, so that you may not fall under condemnation.

JAMES 5:12b

Pastor Elizabeth was a new seminary graduate called to a church in a small city. At the first meeting in the autumn of the city's ministerial fellowship, she was surprised, and somewhat flattered, to be invited to preach at the community Thanksgiving Eve service. Accepting this invitation would mean that she would have to write two sermons that week as well as prepare for Advent, but she agreed. She assumed the other ministers in town must have thought she did a good job at the Thanksgiving Eve service because, some months later, she was asked to preach at the community Good Friday service. And again, Elizabeth accepted this invitation in spite of the busyness of that time of the church year.

A new minister came to another congregation in that city during the following summer, and Elizabeth discovered that he was asked to preach at the Thanksgiving Eve service. Later, he was asked to preach at the Good Friday service as well. And then she understood the unspoken rule of the ministerial association: the new kid on the block is always asked to preach the community services so that the veterans would be spared having to do so. This custom was a rite of passage for new pastors, and had nothing to do with their abilities in the pulpit. Elizabeth learned well the lesson of this practice of which she was not informed.

Too Many Opportunities

Pastor Elizabeth's experience is but one example of how pastors new to congregations and communities can end up too busy with activities beyond the work of the local church. It is not just ministerial associations which so conspire. Community agencies and boards, service clubs, public school committees, fund-raising drives, and cultural associations, to name but a few, may well ask a minister who is new in the community to serve. Their assumption is that, being new, he has few commitments outside the congregation and thus has the time to offer. And, of course, invitations to serve are always extended with the suggestion that such service will be a good way to get to know the community. Opportunities to pray at the opening of city council meetings or to give the invocation at community events like building dedications or Memorial Day parades will be encountered regularly. The temptation of the new pastor, born of a desire to fit in and have a place in the community, is often to agree to too many of these invitations.

In addition to these possibilities for involvement outside the congregation, representatives of denominational governing bodies may also eagerly approach the new pastor, subtly suggesting it is important for him to get involved with committees at that level of the church's life. These, depending on the nature of the work, can also be time consuming. The new pastor will often feel pressured to be a "team player" in this arena as well. Because denominational service can sometimes bring supportive relationships with other pastors, they are particularly tempting to the new pastor.

Too many commitments beyond the congregation to which the pastor has been called inevitably take time away from the work of serving and leading the congregation itself. Towards a pastor who is overinvolved beyond its walls, members of the congregation may begin to feel, if not express, "But what about us? We hired you. We pay you. But you're everywhere but here!" To a certain extent, they are right.

Furthermore, if the time away from the congregation's life doesn't come at the expense of the congregation, it will most likely come from the pastor's family or personal time. So, new pastors need to limit their activities outside the congregation, not only to make sure they are taking care of business at church and at home, but also as a way of modeling good stewardship of their time.

Limiting Outside Commitments

New ministers do well to commit, at least initially, to no more than one community service activity and one denominational responsibility beyond their congregation. And they should ask themselves which one of the many choices available to them will give them a chance to make a real difference, which one will use their gifts well (as opposed to just filling a vacancy), and which one will fit the pastor's vision of what ministry is to be about.

After her lesson in the ministerial association's unspoken rules, Pastor Elizabeth wisely decided to be much more selective about where and to what she would give her time outside the congregation. This meant both prayerful consideration of opportunities that came her way, and saying "yes" and "no" clearly when making her decisions known. She chose to serve on the city housing board where she could address issues regarding fair housing practices towards renters, since this was a matter she cared about strongly having been a renter herself for a number of years. She felt it was a significant extension of her faith commitment to social justice. She also chose to serve on her denomination's women in ministry task force, both as a source of nurture for herself and as a place where she could offer her new pastor experience to others.

Pastor Elizabeth also made clear to her congregation that, with the exception of her clergy support group, these were the only two commitments she would undertake beyond the congregation in order that she could do them well, not spread herself too thin, and fulfill her primary commitment as their pastor. She affirmed that she would not accept any other outside commitments until one of those in which she was currently involved had come to an end. With these announcements, Elizabeth made clear she was going to be available to the members of her congregation, and she modeled being a good steward of her time and abilities.

There are exceptions to this commandment. There are contexts in which a new pastor may not be approached with multiple or significant opportunities for community involvement. These contexts would include rural and small town settings in particular. In such places, longevity of service is often taken as a measure of commitment and is valued more highly than skills or availability. In such a setting, it may be some years before a minister is asked to serve on a board or committee or agency that has real influence. In these cases, the community is simply living by its norms and waiting to see if the minister plans to be around for a significant period of time before invitations are extended. In such a context, the new pastor needs to take care not to try to impose himself upon the community too eagerly. Trying too hard to be part of the local social and political system early on may preclude achieving meaningful involvement later. An exception to this exception is the very small town whose future existence is in question. Such a community may need the leadership abilities and fresh ideas a new pastor brings to help it secure a future for itself. Here, some of the pastor's most crucial work may be in helping the community of which the church is a part to survive.

A NEW PASTOR'S first responsibility is to the congregation that has issued the invitation to be in ministry with them. There will always be plenty to do within that congregation, tasks that should not be neglected even for worthy causes in the larger community.

· IX ·

Thou Shalt Remember What Thy Job Is

*The gifts Christ gave were that some would be
. . . pastors . . . to equip the saints for the work
of ministry, for building up the body of Christ,
until all of us come to the unity of the faith, and
of the knowledge of the Son of God, to maturity
to the measure of the full stature of Christ.*

EPHESIANS 4:11-13

Because the fruits of much ministerial labor are not often concrete, pastors may be tempted to do all manner of work in an attempt to see at least one well-defined end product. But ministers who find themselves shoveling snow, folding worship bulletins, setting up tables and chairs, and emptying wastebaskets have lost sight of their essential tasks, and are simply casting about for a task that has a clearly defined beginning and end. A new pastor succeeding such a "do-it-all" pastor will have to be particularly clear about his job description lest the congregation assume he will simply continue his predecessor's practice of trying to do everything, at the expense of his unique calling.

75

Beyond the pastor's calling to proclaim the gospel in word and deed, his primary responsibilities are two: he is the resident theologian; and he is to equip the people to carry out those ministries suited to their gifts, individually and corporately. It is up to the new pastor to clarify, usually again and again, that these are his jobs. Should he fail to do so, the congregation will impose another image on him or he will drift into an image of ministry that does not facilitate the accomplishment of his unique work.

The Matter of Image

New pastors, indeed all pastors, cannot avoid projecting an image of how they understand themselves and their work. These images can be good or bad, a help or hindrance, to ministry. Some pastors represent themselves as the suffering servant — overworked and always deadly serious about the life-giving gospel. Others, late in their careers, come off as cynics who are merely hanging on until blessed retirement. Bereft of passion, they can drag others into their bitter or apathetic worldview. Some pastors present themselves as the super Christian as compared to the neophytes in faith who make up the congregation. Their "be-like-me" attitude suppresses growth in faith as others are denied the opportunity to discover their unique gifts and identity as children of God. The flip side of that image is the "aw shucks" pastor who conveys the impression that he has no more insight into the faith than anyone else in the congregation. His lack of leadership, born of a desire to fit in at all costs, will set the congregation adrift. And some pastors appear to be nothing more than "hale fellows well met" for whom the faith is little more than a pleasant addition to a life already quite satisfactory.

All of these less than helpful images are born of a failure to be clear about what the pastor's job is. Lack of role clarity by the new pastor means she will drift into one of these false images or allow the congregation to impose an image of their own preference. This matters greatly because it is unavoidable that the pastor will, over time, tend to recreate the church, to a certain extent, in her own image. If the pastor is highly committed to mission work, it is likely the church's commitment to mission will grow over the course of her pastorate. If he is committed to welcoming marginalized people, the congregation will likely become more diverse during his tenure. If she is clearly faithful in following spiritual disciplines, members of the congregation are likely to begin exploring this aspect of the faith. If he is an active teacher and learner, the congregation will probably come to value Christian education more highly.

This shaping of the congregation does not have to be highly structured or forced. It is simply the case that those members who are at odds with the new pastor's style (though not enough so to cause significant conflict) will drift away or become less active while those who find the new pastor's style attractive and nourishing will be drawn to the church or become more active.

Pastor Dan came to a new congregation, following a pastor whose preaching had been dominated by images and illustrations taken primarily from the world of sports and the military. Dan's predecessor had been reasonably successful in several areas of ministry, and had a reputation for taking dramatic actions in the church's life. He was widely known as a family man, and was very active in community and church athletic programs. Large scale building projects and associated fund-raising drives had been frequent, and were enthusiastically pursued and generally successful.

Dan's style was significantly different. Highly gifted in pastoral work, he reached out to many people whose needs seem to have been somewhat overlooked in recent years. His preaching was imaginative, rich and diverse in its imagery and language. He did not cast the Christian faith in terms of a contest or competition, but in terms of a journey and a community. Working with the church's governing board, Dan sought to identify opportunities to serve those living in the church's neighborhood, and helped establish an after-school tutoring program for elementary school age children. Within his first year, a number of families who had been quite active previously lowered their participation level (e.g., dropping off committees) although they continued to be reasonably friendly towards Dan and attended worship fairly regularly. At the same time, several other families and quite a number of single people became more active. And the church received a significant number of new members, including a number of single-parent families.

This type of change is not at all unusual, and is not necessarily either good or bad. It is simply a result of the pastor's image, style, and self-understanding shaping the life of the congregation. Problems arise only when new pastors are not clear about their work as theologians and equippers for ministry because the congregation may become confused or anxious; or when the new pastor deliberately or manipulatively sets out to re-create the church in his own image, conveying none too subtly that those who do not share his vision of how to be Christian may leave. Of course, the impact of the pastor's role understanding takes place within the limits of cultural change for the congregation (see commandment number one).

Resident Theologian

With academic training not only as a preacher and biblical interpreter but also as a theologian, the new pastor brings the competence needed to help the congregation order its life, not according to how other social institutions function, but according to who God is and what God desires from and for the people of God. Congregational members undertake all manner of tasks — managing resources, running programs, resolving conflict, setting goals, raising and disbursing funds, educating members, volunteering in mission projects. They do this work bringing their experience at such tasks in other, nonchurch, settings. A board member from the world of business may be tempted to see the solution to the church's financial problems in terms of getting more members to generate more revenue, and needs to be reminded by the resident theologian that God has called the church to understand itself and its members in something other than such utilitarian and materialistic terms. The board member who is a school principal accustomed to making fairly unilateral decisions may need to be reminded by the resident theologian that God has called the church as a covenant community where decision making is shared. A board member who is not accustomed to having her input taken seriously by virtue of race, gender, class, or employment, may need to be reminded by the resident theologian that each person is the beloved child of God whose gifts and insights are needed by the community of faith. The task of the pastor as resident theologian is not only to preach and teach the faith, but also to help the church be the church, distinct from other institutions, in terms of how it sees its members and their work.

Equipper for Ministry

In addition to proclaiming the gospel and being the resident theologian, the pastor's job is to equip the people for ministry. It is, of course, not only the pastor who has been called by God to use his God-given gifts in ministry. In their baptism, all God's people share this calling. The Christian church believes that God has gifted each person with talents and capacities which find their best use and bestow their greatest joy by being offered in the service of God. A new pastorate offers the opportunity for congregational members to take a fresh look at who they are, as individuals and as a community. The new pastor takes the opportunity to equip the people for ministry by first helping them discern what their gifts and needs are.

Upon arriving at her new congregation, Pastor Martha discovered the congregation had several families that had adopted children. No activity or ministry had ever coalesced around these people. Martha gathered the adoptive parents together and got them talking about their experience in adopting children, and in raising them. The parents enjoyed sharing their stories, and quickly moved to asking one another for help with issues such as handling a child's desire to contact her birth mother. Martha began asking what these parents might do as a group out of their shared faith and shared experience. Quite quickly, they decided to begin regular and open meetings for support of adoptive parents and to provide information on adoption for prospective parents. They brought in a psychologist to speak to them, and also to be a resource for their children. They monitored legislative changes affecting adoption. They taught an adult Sunday school class on adoption as a ministry of loving God's children in need. Word of the group spread to the larger community, and soon couples not from the church began to contact it. A partnering program was established, matching an experienced adoptive couple with a newly adoptive couple. In short, a ministry was born, prompted by Martha's discernment of their common experience and her work to help them see it as a gift for ministry.

Similarly, Pastor Paul found there were several families in his new congregation that had suffered the tragic death of a child, some recently, some many years in the past. Again, no group or ministry had ever come out of this experience. Paul invited the bereaved parents together. Although some were reluctant, and some flatly refused the invitation, several couples did come to the gathering. Paul talked about their common experience and the place of grief in the Christian life. Stories began to be shared, often with many tears. But everyone understood one another's pain. Slowly, gently, with great pastoral sensitivity, Paul asked what they, with God's help, might do with their particular experience of loss. Initially, the group decided to meet simply to support one another by listening and by being available to one another whenever the need to talk about a deceased child came upon one of them. Soon they began remembering anniversaries of deaths and approached those who had chosen not to come to explain their work. The occasion came when members of the group were able to companion other parents, both within and without the congregation, who suffered this terrible loss.

The Reverend Ruth had a knack for doing equipping for ministry work with individuals. One woman she counseled was a new grandmother who was saddened because her beloved first grandchild lived several states away. The woman despaired of the infrequency with which she got to see the child. The joy she experienced whenever she did get to see her granddaughter gave way to deep sadness when she returned home from a visit. Ruth learned this woman had kept the church kitchen cleaned up for many years — washing the dish towels, buying supplies, cleaning the refrigerator — and that she no longer seemed to find satisfaction in this task. She had simply done it for a long time, and everyone assumed she always would.

Ruth asked her if she would try working in the church nursery one Sunday morning. At first she protested that she was too old and that it was a job to be shared among the children's parents. But with a little persuasion from Ruth, the woman did take a morning in the nursery and had a wonderful time. Being with the little ones, so reminiscent of her granddaughter, was a blessing. She was great with the kids. And she came back again and again. Parents left their little ones utterly confident they would be lovingly cared for. The grandmother even took a community college class on infant and toddler development, and began sitting for children one night a week at the domestic assault shelter. And someone else started cleaning the kitchen.

Discerning who is in the congregation, what their experiences, needs, and gifts are, and imagining ways these could be offered to God in doing a work that needs to be done is the essence of equipping people for ministry. It is a work that can be done with individuals, with groups, even with a whole congregation. Discerning a need in the community in which the church is located — for housing, for medical care, for care for the aging — and mobilizing the church to meet that need if it is gifted to do so is nothing more than equipping for ministry done on a larger scale. The benefits are the same — people grow in faith through their service, and very often find joy by bringing joy to the heart of God through the right use of their gifts.

PREACHER, THEOLOGIAN, equipper for ministry. These are the unique tasks of the minister. Neglected, the congregation will lose its way and miss many an opportunity for life-giving ministry. And the pastor will be living out of an unworthy alternative image for ministry. Attended to, these tasks will empower the congregation and its members to find clarity about their callings. And the pastor will be freed to do what she is best gifted to do. A favorite Arab proverb of mine says that if you do not know where you are going, any road will take you there. Remembering what our job is will allow the church to find the path of glorifying God through satisfying and meaningful ministry.

Being the resident theologian and equipping people for ministry through the discernment of gifts as well as opportunities for their use are primary roles for the minister.

If they are lost among trivial jobs that could well be taken care of by other hands, the minister's unique and godly contribution to the life of Christ's church will be lost. And the price will be paid by the kingdom of God.

Thou Shalt Not Commit Adultery

Jesus said, "When the Son of Man comes in his glory, and all the angels with him, then he will sit on the throne of his glory. All the nations will be gathered before him, and he will separate people from one another as a shepherd separates the sheep from the goats."

MATTHEW 25:31-32

So much has been written in recent years about the tragedies wrought through clergy sexual misconduct that nothing else need be added here on that subject. If clergy have not gotten the message by now, they have either chosen not to or vainly believe themselves to be the exception to the rules governing contact between pastor and parishioner. The consequences of either can be devastating.

This last commandment for new pastors does not have to do with adultery in the sexual sense, but rather in the sense of the word "adulterate," the mixing together of two things that do not belong together. Sexual adultery is certainly an example of adulteration, one in which two people who should not be involved with one another are

85

so involved. But there are other examples of adulteration that occur in ministry, and it is to these this chapter speaks. How shall we be in, but not of, this world? How shall we distinguish, and keep separate, the sheep-like from the goat-like in our ministry?

As previously mentioned, the new pastor will often be confronted with a number of requests for community involvement upon arrival in the new community. Some guidelines for making wise choices have already been suggested. Beneath all such choices is the question, "What am I baptizing by my participation?" In other words, the minister's presence and participation in some activities will convey to others that the activity or organization is, at some level, "Christian." If this were not the case, the good reverend would not be there lending his support. This perceptual problem can raise its head with regard to this tenth commandment.

Shortly after arriving at this new pastorate, the Reverend James was asked to join in a rotation of pastors who prayed at the opening of city commission meetings. This seemed to Jim a good and not very taxing way to make his presence known in the community, to make contact with some of the powers that be, and to give the impression that he was a team player. And so, over the next few months, Jim took a regular turn praying as the council began its meetings. Some months later, a divisive issue arose in the community having to do with the siting of a waste disposal facility. It appeared that the facility would be located in a low-income section of town on the site of an abandoned factory, although a number of sites were considered suitable. It would provide few jobs since it was to be highly automated, and the owners assured the community it would not be a source of significant pollution. The neighborhood residents, however, were neither happy nor convinced, and voiced opposition to locating the facility near their homes. They asked that the abandoned factory property be converted instead into a park and playground for their neighborhood since none existed.

Pastor Jim felt he must speak in solidarity with the community's poorest citizens. He appeared before the council and asked for a delay in the decision, for further consideration of alternative sites, and for attention to be given to the neighborhood request for a park. During a break in the council's deliberations, one of the council members chided Jim in front of several others, saying it seemed sometimes Jim came to bless the council's work and now had come to question their judgment. "Which way is it going to be, Reverend?" Jim realized that in this council member's eyes, he had previously baptized the work of the council, and thereby compromised his ability to speak freely and critically when his voice was needed. The council's rule seemed to be that it was perfectly all right for pastors to pray, but that if they did so, they should stay out of public issues.

Similar problems can arise if a pastor joins a particular service club or country club or moves in certain social circles at the exclusion of others. A new minister everyone agreed was an outstanding preacher and an exceptionally capable administrator finally was forced out of his church because of the widely held perception that he catered to the most affluent members and did not give equal attention to all the baptized. The minister protested this simply was not so. But when he left, he took a segment of the congregation with him to his new congregation, a segment that included most of the more affluent members.

This is certainly not to say that pastors must stay out of all community activities and have no friends in the church. It is to say that pastors need to take some thought for what they choose to do and with whom in terms of public perception. For the sake of their freedom to speak the truth in love on behalf of the dispossessed and for the sake of their calling to serve all members with compassion, this must be so.

New pastors may also be confronted with congregational pressures for quick results in dealing with long-standing problems. The desired "results" often might be more members, greater attendance at worship, or larger receipts. In addition to the erroneous notion that it is up to the new pastor to achieve these results quickly and on her own, these pressures can tempt the pastor to use methods and techniques purported to produce results but which are not compatible with the gospel. Yes, there are ways to get more members, some of which use the least appealing aspects of mass marketing and manipulation. Yes, giving can be increased through the application of unrelenting pressure on members, but is this a biblical model? Again, in our drivenness to achieve results, we must take care what we baptize. The Reverend Ernest T. Campbell once suggested that we dangerously deceive ourselves if we believe we can use the techniques of Madison Avenue to speak of the Via Dolorosa without seriously compromising the latter. Not only our goals in ministry, but also the means by which we seek to reach them, must comport with what we believe lest we mix that which does not belong together.

This baptism of methods which only serve to adulterate can also occur in the adoption of secular therapies for use in ministry. In our eagerness to be effective and make a good impression at the outset of our pastorate, we may be tempted to embrace the latest therapeutic approach or spiritual fad, rather than do the patient work of pastoral care and the cure of souls. Such chasing after what appears to work quickly will usually come at the expense of the pastor's unique ability to ask parishioners such questions as where God is in the midst of the issue with which they are struggling, what they are being asked to let die, what newness God is seeking to bring to life in them, and how this can be brought to God in prayer. Is the pastor's goal to adopt the latest pop therapeutic technique that seeks to adjust people to a fallen world, or is it to empower people to participate in their own transformation, and that of the world, by the grace of God?

Similarly, it is easy for new pastors to be drawn into community social or political issues by having certain positions labeled as "Christian." Pastors are surely called to speak prophetically, both within and without the church, but this must be done sparingly (on "blue chip" issues), with prayer and with shared consideration of the issue. Jumping unthinkingly on the bandwagon of a partisan position (of a party in the church or in the community) as if social issues are simple and as if good Christians cannot be on opposing sides leads to the erosion of pastoral credibility. New pastors need to take care that in their eagerness to fit in to their new community, they do not unwittingly get signed up for some cause they have not fully considered.

Obedience to this commandment is nothing more

than checking in regularly to see if what we are saying and doing actually coheres with what we believe. In other words, are we being the theologian in residence about our own work? A new pastor who started an investment club in his church was somehow surprised to find many of his congregation thought that he was more interested in the stock market than in God. What did Jesus say about serving mammon and God? A similar impression is conveyed by the pastor who haggles for every nickel of compensation, far beyond the bounds of ensuring just pastoral compensation. At a meeting on clergy compensation, one minister after another rose to discuss the implications of various proposals with regard to the regulations of the Internal Revenue Service. At last, one of the saints of that assembly rose to say he wondered if anyone there gathered knew as much about furthering the kingdom of God as they did about the regulations of the Internal Revenue Service? Those who had ears, heard.

Some pastors convey the impression that the focus of their ministry is not on serving God and others, but on always getting their way, on winning every battle. Others serve the god of being well liked. We do not all have to be saints, working for a pittance, never asserting ourselves, always giving way to others. But our words and actions need to be grounded in the gracious God whose call to ministry has shaped us. Otherwise, we will mix in worship of some other, lesser god — power, money, affirmation, what works most quickly. And we will have committed adultery.

SOME ACTIONS ARE simply incompatible with ministry. Baptizing with our words or presence certain groups or ideas or positions will eventually limit our freedom to proclaim the truth that is in us. Adopting certain techniques from the culture in which we live without critically assessing their compatibility with our faith may lead us to surrender our distinctive role in, and ability to speak to, that culture. Acting out of our financial anxieties or need for accomplishment at the expense of service will undermine our credibility as a servant calling others to join in service. Moses had it right when he led off the Ten Commandments with "Thou shalt have no other gods before me" (Exodus 20:3). That bespeaks the adultery of which we must be most careful.

The Eleventh Commandment

"Lord, to whom can we go?"

JOHN 6:68a

The ministry is an enormously stressful vocation, and aside from major congregational conflict, a new pastorate is the most stressful period in that already stressful vocation. Too many roles, too many hours, too many expectations, too little affirmation can all increase the stress load of the new pastor. The stress of a new pastorate can drive us away from what matters most in ministry, and send us down all manner of less than helpful paths. Not only new pastors, but all pastors, are prone to getting into trouble when they attempt to go it alone. Perspective on problems gets warped, the range of alternative approaches for everything from biblical interpretation to programming becomes truncated, and the tendency towards that most destructive of all emotions — self-pity — looms large.

Having a wise and experienced mentor is a partial, but crucial, antidote for these problems. In some denominational governing bodies or regional administrative units, a mentor for each new pastor may be routinely appointed.

If this is not the case, a pastor new to a congregation will be wise to seek one out. Most often, but certainly not always, a mentor will come from one's own faith tradition. And it is most helpful if the mentor has experience with the type of church and community in which the new pastor is serving.

Having found a mentor, it is important to meet with him or her regularly, at least once each month, particularly in the first year of a new pastorate. The mentor's value is not only in suggesting alternatives and sharing resources, but most essentially in bearing burdens, giving honest feedback, and being unabashedly in the new pastor's corner. The best mentors are far better listeners than speakers.

A good mentor needs, first of all, to be secure in himself, comfortable with his gifts, and not threatened by those of others. Good mentors will not rely heavily on the advice of "do it the way I do it" nor be so caught up in the demands of their own work that they cannot be fully present to those with whom they consult. It is helpful if mentors are experienced pastors so that a situation of two pastors stumbling about in blindness or sharing mutual ignorance does not prevail.

It is tempting to believe that after one has served a couple of different congregations in different contexts one knows full well how to begin a new pastorate and will not benefit much by having a mentor. This temptation to believe in the sufficiency of one's own experience is usually deadly. Even if the new pastor has been called to a large, prestigious church, and thereby had her experience, giftedness, and skill seemingly validated, it is still more than wise to have a mentor with whom to share the struggles of ministering in a new place with new people and new problems.

It is striking to me that Jesus' first act of ministry, before any word of teaching or deed of healing, was to gather to himself a community. He called to himself a group of men and women who would make his life-transforming journey with him. He did not "go it alone" but sought to share the richness and complexity of his ministry with others. If the One who did not need a human mentor put himself in relationship with others with whom he could share the challenges and defeats, the puzzlement and the moments of insight, the conflicts and the joys of mysterious communion with God, should we as new pastors not go and do likewise?